AMERICAN CONTRABANDO

Larry Unger

Edited by LC Unger

PAGE PUBLISHING
Conneaut Lake, PA

First originally published by Page Publishing 2023

ISBN 979-8-88654-492-3 (pbk)
ISBN 979-8-88654-494-7 (digital)

CONTENTS

Preface...v
Chapter 1: Beach to Site Six Flight 1
Chapter 2: Growing in Orange County............................... 19
Chapter 3: Living in North County.................................... 33
Chapter 4: Searching for PV 45
Chapter 5: Pirates Attack.. 63
Chapter 6: Oaxaca Express 81
Chapter 7: Terminal Island Life.. 99
Chapter 8: Thai Sticks to New York 114
Chapter 9: I Found a Gold Mine...................................... 127
Chapter 10: A Plane to Jamaica.. 139
Chapter 11: Return from Jamaica...................................... 157
Chapter 12: Landing on a Bridge 176
All Pictures 197

PREFACE

This book is about a young man who grew up in Anaheim, Orange County, California, during the 1950s, 1960s and 1970s. He was looking for adventure. That would include danger money and freedom from a few archaic class one drug laws. He got involved with a group of kids he knew from school in Anaheim who moved to Laguna Beach that were selling LSD, marijuana, and Afghan hash. He knew that Mexico is the closest country anyone could purchase large quantities of marijuana. He went there and liked it, found the Wild West. He lived there for two years. He established the sunshine ranch near Lake Chapala, making connections that he could have never made without having large amounts of LSD sunshine. He rocked their little world, selling and giving away large amounts of sunshine little orange barrel-type pills. It was legal in Mexico at that time. Last time he heard about the tabbing machine, it was in Chuck's desert house.

He is very much against using hard drugs. He believes marijuana is a much safer medicine to use for any discomfort like pain mentally or physically. He thinks LSD and marijuana could be used to stop the use of heroin. The thing about LSD most people do not know is that every time you use LSD it becomes less effective, the colors will fade, and after a few days, it's no big deal. LSD is like any other drug; if you take too much ibuprofen at one time, it will kill you. After a while, you will just get tired of LSD. He claims both drugs were not addictive, and he knows because he has used them fifty years ago. The one reason he stays away from opioids is that he knows it's not easy to stop using those and sometimes never. He has never used a needle and never will because he has seen the harm and deaths it has done to his friends. Everything started to break up when some of the brothers started smuggling and fooling around with cocaine.

What sunshine LSD did for him was exploded his mind and showed him what is in his brain. Wow, what power it has and unlocked it, and it makes him want to see all these things naturally by taking care of his body, exercising, eating the right foods, and doing good deeds with good thoughts, all without moving to Tibet. He would secretly call his flight service at the airport "Medicine without Borders."

He started smuggling marijuana with motorcycles and then used that money to buy a large sailboat, the Kona Mauri. He built two 55' concrete boats in Mexico and imported one full of weed. Then he used that money to buy airplanes. He has covered thousands of air miles and thousands of sea miles carrying tons of weed; every trip could be a suicide trip he has been chased in the air on the ground and at sea. He was attempted to be boarded by Mexican pirates on the high seas and averted by his military training and an AR-15. He crashed airplanes in other countries. He did things with airplanes that the airplane manuals say you can't do. Stolen airplanes opened a drug route from Texas through Yucatan to Jamaica. He would put you on the seat of a motorcycle racing across the high desert at night. The helm of the KONA MAURI ketch sailing up the coast of Mexico with tons of marijuana and riding in the copilots, seat loaded with marijuana racing over the 600 miles of sea between Texas and Yucatan at one hundred feet, looking into the cabs of oil rigs and waving at the workers, and them waiving back.

Is it just divine intervention or more likely luck? When the Internal Revenue Special Investigation unit steps in, it's not good, no luck here. It had to be the two airplanes, a yacht, ranches, homes, and all the jet charters around the country. The worst visit was Timothy Leary at the Idyllwild ranch. Turn on, tune in, and get rich. No dropping out. That was when he was a fugitive like his brothers, and he was finally captured after a $125,000 arrest warrant is issued. Then he went to prison after a couple of years of legal fighting. He opened a drug route into the prison to bring in kilos of weed after he was released from prison after only six months. He bought a new airplane and opened a flight service at a local beach airport, then reopened Medicine without Borders again, and started paying his taxes. The large flow of weed into California and Canada began again.

Then after a couple of years of being dogged by the Fed police, his lawyers told him he should move out of California. The feds have told them to tell him that for his health, he should move way out of state. The attorneys were getting their information from a retired assistant Federal attorney who rubs elbows and talks to all the Fed cops. His wife had cancer and needed marijuana for her health reasons, like eating and enjoying life a little; he fixes that. He gives him a full-pressed wrapped kilo rattling around in a briefcase in the hallway of the San Diego Federal Courthouse. The attorney's jaw dropped when he opened and peeked into the case and hugged it lightly not to be noticed. Now he said this attorney and George Chula are like brothers to him. Chula had his DUI reduced to reckless driving for only $25K. He had both of their home phone numbers, and he calls them a lot. His whole thing is that he would never bring hard narcotics into the USA that ruin so many people's lives—millions. It is easier to find heroin, and it is cheaper to buy than good marijuana in some states. He claims that is how he lasted so long in the game and he is alive today because he never smuggled hard narcotics.

Several of his partners have been murdered, died in drug plane crashes, or tortured by Mexican soldiers, and/or police all for a weed. George Chula told him that an assistant Federal attorney told him he should move from his Valley Center Ranch as he could get shot. The Federal agents are having marital problems being away at night watching him for over a year. It's hard to watch somebody twenty-four seven who lives on a ranch, with no place to get coffee and doughnuts. Almost immediately after hearing from his attorneys about the second threat from the feds, he told his brothers, and they didn't seem to be worried about it.

These Federals are very serious people, and they do shoot people. For them to warn him was unheard of. Then he moved from his ranch the next day, took two airplanes, a large truck full of furniture, cars, and pickups, then moved to the Pittsburgh area after several trips, to a town with an airport but no air service. He opened an air taxi company and a tire store, and suddenly hundreds of pounds of weed started turning up there. Then his house was burned down suspiciously along with the large tire dealer's facility that had been helping him build his tire business and selling weed. Now he had enough legal flying time built up to get a job, flying turbine engine airplanes in New York.

Then after flying a few years in New York, he bought a farm in Iowa and moved there to raise his family and flew for a regional airline. Also he started a construction company that builds and remodels homes and raised Black Angus cattle at his ranch/farm in Iowa. Then when he was too old to fly airlines, he moved to Florida. He worked another eighteen years at a large simulator company teaching and certifying pilots to fly Learjets while flying freight all over the USA, Mexico, and the Caribbean part-time.

When he got tired of working full-time, he moved to Daytona Beach to ride his Harley-Davidson Road Glide motorcycle, dancing, writing articles about flying and books about sailing flying, and smuggling with great getaways from the law. The law only wanted to catch him with a load. He has never been caught with any drugs on him that he couldn't eat. He has never been questioned about anything and not even for tax evasion the case that stuck. He spent time breaking into in Hollywood elite; it didn't take long with his stash. His Mexican friends or mano's had friends in Hollywood that introduced him to some of the actors and musicians. He had all the best drugs they loved him. He partied with the Carradine brothers. David invited him to his house and to Paramount Studios to work. Then he was introduced to Arthur Lee. Arthur took him to Paramount Recording studios Whisky a Go-Go and let him stay at his guesthouse when he was in Los Angeles. Then one day, he put a whistle around his neck and hired him to be his manager. Then there was an incident with his Walther PPK that ended it. He had to get back to ranch life and his horses.

CHAPTER 1

Beach to Site Six Flight

I purchased this factory hopped-up Aero Commander 680S twin-engine airplane. 680 stands for the largest cabin-class airplane that North American aircraft built. The S stands for Supercharged. They mostly build fighter airplanes, like the P-51 Mustang and jet fighter aircraft. These airplanes are built tough. You can bounce them around some and not get hurt just like fighter aircraft. They can take it!

Back in the day, you could buy larger-horsepower airplanes from manufactures just as the large car companies sell their high-performance cars. They are Hot Rods also. It's really no big deal, nuts and bolts. The only difference in the appearance of the Aero Commander from the stock models that you could see was the engine cowlings; they are a little larger than the stock, so the root-type superchargers could be enclosed in the larger cowlings.

The name of this aircraft was NOVEMBER FIVE SEVEN FIVE THREE SIERRA. It loved the Sierras. I loved all the valleys and canyons in the Sierras. I knew them like the back of my hand. I learned to fly around Southern California and Arizona, specifically Western Arizona. I flew around these mountains, beaches, and deserts every day. I could stay below mostly all California radars; remember I said mostly.

I would always like to read the NTSB National Transportation Safety Board California accident reports to see if there are any aircraft or pilots that I know of may have crashed. It could be some bad weather or pilot error to blame, and most importantly, I might learn something. After a few years, I sold this airplane, and it turned up on the NTSB accident report. It was in a bad accident. It crashed in Upland California West of the Beaumont Banning pass California in 1977, and it killed five people. The actual report is blocked by the NTSB for some reason. The window gives a number. I think I do not have authorization to access that NTSB number if I wanted to. I just hope it wasn't shot down for mistaken identity.

This is a fast-slippery airplane only for highly experienced pilots who should fly it, like Bob Hoover and me. What I liked about this airplane is its big fat main tires and a large front wheel with power steering. This aircraft is designed for soft field landings. They do not advertise it as insurance rates would probably skyrocket. This does not bother me as I never insured my airplanes anyway and never registered them. I just keep the bill of sale, and in case I was ever confronted, I would show the bill of sale and say I haven't had time to register it.

I never was confronted about any aircraft ownership. Also, if it is found all banged up and unflyable in or on some pasture or airport in any other country, or in one case, one of my planes was found on a boulevard in Galveston, Texas, on the gulf coast. It was full of pot and empty of gas and papers.

When asked, the FAA would open a file on the incident and wait for something to come in like a hard copy. If nothing comes in, it will not be continued; they already have too many accidents to investigate, where they have a good name and address, and then they would say we are working on it. They do not have my information. It is always one of my aliases I use. The beach is somewhere in the middle of the hard and soft fields. Sometimes you need an airplane with a lot of ground clearance in order to taxi around rocks and soft sand. This is not the Commander; it is real low to the ground as ten inches from the ground the bottom is like a sled. It is really fast; that's better for me.

I would have all the paint worn off with some dents in the belly of this airplane after a few flights. What's cool is that you would have to lie on the ground to see the damage. I would use an airplane with more ground clearance for the rough fields like King Airs in the mountains. This aircraft had a fairly new paint job—orange and dark brown stripes over tan. It looked almost like new. It looked like it cost a lot more money than it cost. The reason they were not popular was that several of them have had bad crashes.

I think mostly because of pilot error. These are high-power supercharged engines, and when you operate them in high cold altitudes, like ISA minus thirty degrees way below zero, you have to operate the throttles with the tips of your fingers—no sudden movements so you do not cool the engines to fast. If you do, the top of the pistons blows off and the fuel ejection systems start spraying 120 octane fuel into the wing and fire erupts and the spar melts, wing falls off, and you can take the thought from there. Not anything good will happen.

The few people who liked the Commanders was because of the speeds; they would reach nearly propjet cruise speeds and close to the same max speeds as the propjets. That is exactly what I needed a plane faster than any jet helicopters and an airplane that can land at 1,000 feet. This airplane can land on thousands of runways that jets can't use for landing because the runways are too short.

I paid $25,000 at one of the larger aircraft dealers at the Van Nuys Airport near Hollywood. They were asking $45,000. I made my offer of $25,000. They looked a little puzzled. One had just crashed in Northern California. I reminded them of that and the other crashes the Aero Commanders have had. Then I told them I had done several hours of research on this aircraft model and this was all it was worth now, and I had the cash with me. I started to walk out, and the mood changed!

They invited me into a large plush office. I walked in with the salesmen I was working with, and inside behind a large hand-carved desk was the owner of the company. I was introduced while an outstanding secretary with long blond hair, green eyes, and a British accent walked in and asked if I wanted anything to drink. I said I would like a cup of coffee. She looked a little disappointed as maybe she would have been more happy if I had said a bottle of champagne.

The owner of the company was a famous pilot, and I am sure he has dealt with most of the large movie stars as they keep their airplanes here at his hanger complex on the Van Nuys Airport. We talked about airplanes and movies. His airplanes have easy-to-identify tail numbers. I have seen them in many movies. There are several tail numbers that are assigned to entertainment companies. I have a list of the tail numbers and use one of them when I have an aircraft repainted. My thinking is that nobody would want to shoot down an airplane and have it all on film. It could be a career-ending event.

He said, "$25,000 cash, please, and I will have the secretary start the paperwork." I opened up my briefcase, and there were several bank-wrapped hundred-dollar bills in $10,000 bundles. I took out three and split one in half and passed them over to the owner. I said I was sorry they do not have $1,000 and $500 bills anymore. I didn't say my crew was partly responsible for it, the war on drugs. He said he was sorry too sometimes they do million-dollar deals and have their bankers come here to count all the money they do it on the large table behind me.

I received all the paperwork, both engine logbooks and the airframe logbooks. I walked out with my mechanic to the aircraft on the ramp. We opened all the doors and most of the inspection plates. We went over everything—engine hours and aircraft hours—and found all the numbers added up and there was no damage or corrosion and decided it was safe to fly. This is going to be fun to see if I can work the navigation radios and the communication radios to at least be cleared to taxi and cleared for takeoff and at least navigate out of the Los Angeles Terminal Control Area without a midair collision or worse an airspace violation.

When I was cleared to takeoff, I lined up on the runway and locked the brakes up as hard as I could, pushing on the top of brake pedals. I set the parking brake and slowly advanced the power levers to max manifold pressure and max engine temperatures. Wow, these engines were screaming. The engines were geared, and the gears made a howling noise along with the short six-inch exhaust stacks, which sounded as if it is going to blow up, but I sat there for a couple of minutes.

I was thinking, *If this widow-maker airplane explodes, let's do it right here and now. They have a fire truck and rescue truck here.* That probably would not have saved me by the time they got out here if it blew up on the runway. I would be a crispy critter before they would arrive. The fuel tanks are mostly above the cabin in the wing tanks—another reason the Aero Commanders were not really popular. There are a couple of hundred gallons of gas over your head. All these crashes are ugly, but the airplanes are really fast.

I was looking at all my engine temperatures, cylinder head oil temp, and pressure. They were all starting to get on the red line. Needless to say, these engines are not designed to make this much power on the ground for a long time. They need to get in the air so they can start breathing. So I quickly released the brakes and hung on. The acceleration was pulling me back on the seat. I did not have much fuel on board as this made us very light. The noise didn't start quieting down until I reached around fifty knots, which only took a moment, and then passing one hundred knots, the noise level started being acceptable.

I have lifted off, and all the shaking and noise was starting to be comfortable. Now I had to clean up my airplane flaps up, gear up, level off at 2,000 feet, and stay below 200 Kts as what the controller requested, and this thing is a racehorse. Then I did the after-takeoff checklist climb and cruse checklist and contact the departure control. I was not used to pulling the power back and still doing 200 Kts.

I called the Los Angeles departure controller a little late, but it was just in time for him to tell me. I was leaving the Los Angeles terminal control area. I already covered about thirty miles. He sounded as if he was glad to see me go as he probably had been watching me on his radar screen and wondering why it was taking me so long to call him after takeoff from Van Nuys Airport for traffic advisories.

I wished him a nice day and changed my frequency as I was heading out toward the dessert passing through the Beaumont Banning Pass into clear air. Beautiful the visibility went from ten miles to one hundred miles. I poured the power to it and climbed to 10,000 and did an aileron roll and turned west toward Palomar Mountain and the coast. I passed south of Palms Springs. Then over Palomar Mountain Observatory, I started a slow decent 200 feet per minute to see how fast she would go. Redline is how fast it will go downhill—close to 300 MPH. I could see the coast now, and I lined up on the runway, called the tower, and landed.

The border patrol only had one plane that could keep up with me except for the jets. The jets were chasing big-time powder smugglers and could not land on short runways. It weighed 25,000 pounds with lots of guns and ammo aboard. It is the Douglas Sky Raider. I wouldn't think they would have one around Southern California, as I have never seen one until this flight. They use them to shoot down cocaine jets coming from Columbia. They can shoot them down for all I care, for all the death and destruction caused by hard narcotics that are killing our kids. A thousand pounds of herbs is worth nothing compared to what a thousand pounds of coke is worth. But the weed is a thousand pounds of medicine that can make people feel good. I am Medicine without Borders.

So what usually the DEA does is chase the coke jets with all the DEA and border patrol jet planes that are just like corporate jets, no gunports. That's why they need the Sky Raiders Six fifty-caliber machine guns. With my military 50 cal experience, I can easily say there is no aircraft I know that would not blow apart after flying through one burst of six rapid-fire fifty-caliber bullets. It would be like hitting a wall of steel at 300 MPH or more.

The jets will follow the suspect cocaine aircraft and try and vector a Sky Raider to intercept it at a place on the map where there are no cities and where a plane crash would probably go unnoticed. Then after the government crash investigation and cleanup team, if the crash is found, the team's initial report would always say that it could be fuel starvation that caused this crash. The accident's final report might say drug plane, might not, might be broken radio plane, might be not found plane.

I always believe the government investigators in all branches of government know who are really responsible for smuggling hard drugs. They will capture someone that's doing pot if the pot people make it easy for them to catch. Some of their kids are having drug problems also so they want to stop the flow of drugs as much as they can. To get down to the nitty-gritty, I think a person would rather smoke a super good joint than jamb a needle into his or her arm. One problem is that it is harder to get good grass than it is to get some smack

I never did see the drug interdiction airplanes in California. They were all over Florida. The drug interdiction pilots would say you are not supposed to see us because we are doing a good job. Later on, after obtaining more flight ratings, I started working only at night, and then I never saw any police.

I do remember one night over Brownsville, Texas, as I was passing through at 400 feet. I picked up a police helicopter on patrol. I wanted to scare him a little, so I passed him close to his tail rotor. I had no lights on. I came out of nowhere. I thought if I disrupted his air around his tail rotor, he might get a rough ride for a moment. I do not know as I could not see behind me. But he gave chase as I could see the red white and blue lights flashing between my engine cowlings and the fuselage. It quickly faded and disappeared behind me as I was hauling ass on my way to central Texas, and there was no way he could catch me now.

I had sent two drivers, surfboards, a huge bad ass dog, and a jacked-up orange four-wheel drive Ford 150 with big tires down to my ranch near Guadalajara. The ranch was perfect. I inherited it from a big-time dealer from San Francisco. I worked with him for a couple years moving around grass. I would fly up to San Francisco and rent warehouses that were next to a railroad spur yard. Like Hayward, California, we called it Wayward.

But anyway, they would send up railroad freight cars loaded to the top with dirty dusty bags of charcoal coal all in brown paper bags with no name. I think the border patrol didn't want to get dirty by searching through them. They didn't have that radar looking through machines at that time. Then I would just fly back to Guadalajara. They had all the distribution things covered. We did this for a while, and then it stopped. Probably they got caught somehow or maybe made too much money and just quit.

Meanwhile back at the ranch, the house was a typical Mexican ranch home. The indoor-outdoor kitchen is in the center as is the living room, and then the bedrooms are on the wings. I always get the west wing. This one had four bedrooms and a guesthouse. The good thing was that it had a twelve-foot wall all around it with a huge high gate that was big enough for a large dump truck to drive in. The garages are out back with the stable. All of the help I had always left at night, and I am sure they would not like anything to happen to their paydays, so whatever happened there, they wouldn't know about or care about it. None of all of this can be seen from the highway.

This is where I kept my horse and Chev Malibu. I didn't need to drive my car for work. My cartel car I would call it was a near new Pontiac GTO. The cartel was like for pot—not that hard shit as far as I know like if you lose a load, you probably won't be murdered? Probably?

A cute story near the ranch is a rather small village we would pass sometimes on the way home from the jungle out buying weed. There was this restaurant and a bar, tables, and umbrellas mostly outside but also inside. They have electricity that mainly means to us cold beer.

One thing you have to understand it's Wild West like man o mano in the jungles and mountains and the police cannot call fifty policemen in a moment's notice like downtown in any city in Mexico. Basically, if there is a chance, they could be out-gunned even a teeny chance they just are as nice as can be and would help you. But as my story goes, we stopped for a beer at this restaurant. We were eating and drinking, and two cops walked up. We were all spread out on different tables, and our hands were above the tables, eating and drinking, and we did not want to act like a threat to them.

The only reason we have the guns is the bandidos in the mountains and jungles, and the cops know that. The bandidos put up roadblocks. Most of these roads up here have only one lane. They are almost impossible to see from the air. If you need two lanes, you break out the machetes and make another lane. Incidentally that's not my style. The bandidos up here rob and kill anyone that can't shoot back.

I smiled at the cop as they walked up and said, "Que pasa."

And he pointed at our guns and started saying, "No que con beber cerveza," and then I realized what was going on. They did not allow anyone to drink with their guns on in a restaurant or bar. I quickly told everyone we should put our guns in the truck while apologizing, and the policeman was almost bowing and backing up apologizing to me.

The truck was all dirty and full of pot. And then they just walked passed it and away as if they have just been a big service to the community. And I started thinking that maybe there have been many gunfights at that restaurant in the past. We placed our guns in the truck, finished dinner and a few more beers, then went back to the Rancho Del Sol to start pressing out kilos.

I would not want to get caught walking around Guadalajara with my gun out. The cops would take my gun away and lock me up and maybe beat me. That holster in the picture is for play. It's fast draw. I have two others, one for inside my waist and one for the boot. If I think I might get searched where I am going, I use the boot clip. I was in the Army for three years. I was trained really well on how to use weapons.

If you dress and look like you have money and if you know the name of a Guadalajara attorney, you will be treated quite well. One day, I was walking out the front door to walk over to a restaurant, as my favorite lawyer pulled up in front of my townhouse in Guadalajara. He pulled over on the wrong side of the boulevard driving his big black Benz to talk for a moment. He closed off half a lane on the one the wrong side of a boulevard. He got out and asked me if I had a joint, and I said I did.

I said, "Step in my condo for a moment." He walked into the entry way and followed me into my den where I had a coffee table with a rolling tray under it and a few joints on it the maid rolled. She said her husband needed it for his back. I told her to roll some and leave some, and I would always have rolled joints. I offered Jose one. He picked it up and held it like a real cigarette between his fingers. They do look a lot like real cigarettes sort of if you don't look closely. As I followed him, we walked out to the curb. There were two policemen standing by his wrong-way-parked car.

They had a ticket pad out. Jose and the cops were talking way too fast for me to understand, but the good part was that they were smiling and laughing and carrying on. Jose is a hand talker. He was waving his hands around with a joint in it, and I was smiling and nodding yes with my head. They both put their ticket book away and left happy with no bite as they say everyone was happy, and we both looked at the unlit joint in his hand and laughed out loud. We had both forgotten he had the joint between his fingers. And I was wondering how much power he had to have those cops not want the morder or the bite as we would say for him parking like wrong way. All these lawyers are all hooked up with the police somehow.

The Rancho Del Sol

Sunshine Ranch

Hippy Vaquero

Back at the sunshine ranch, we worked a lot in the beginning. We had to press all the kilos at my rancho with my crew, which was my American foreman from Reno. He couldn't go home for some reason and lived for free at my ranch with a bonus when the pot is sold, the same for my two kids who are Americans going to medical school. They would be some really cool doctors someday I would bet. I think they would have done it for free for all the weed they could smoke and take home and some cash. This is pretty much old school I learned from the old contrabandists.

I had a log striped of the bark, and we squared it up into three feet long flat on two sides. We cut out two square holes about the size of a pressed kilo. And I had a small hydraulic jack. There was a window in the stable about three feet wide. I would place the log in the window and fill the square holes up with weed and put a board on top and jack it down, load some more, and jack it down again until it felt about right and then weighed it and added or subtracted some, then wrapped it up with the brown paper and red-green or blue cellophane. Some of my Mexican friends always helped me. They had been making these presses for generations. This was not their first press.

After the weed was picked up from my ranch, it was driven to Guaymas, Mexico then the load was ferried across the Sea of Cortez to Santa Rosalea. Then it was driven across the Baja California peninsula to the Pacific side to meet me on the beach. We all had Rolex watches good for one second a year, and since we worked in different time zones, we always stayed on Pacific time. This was going to be my first time landing on the beach with a heavy airplane. So I had Plan B. If I crashed or sunk into the sand, I would ride up the coast with the pot truck, steal another plane, and finish the trip. In my bag were keys to every airplane manufactured in the USA. I landed on a long stretch of beach without an incident. I had enough runway on the beach for a takeoff without turning around.

There was the main north-south highway about a quarter mile east of the beach, with a marshland in between. To get across, you would need four-wheel drive. This was the main road from Tijuana to Cabo San Lucas, the only one at this time. Traffic was slow, but cars and trucks started stopping and watching us.

I told my brother Big John to go out by the wing and fold his big arms look mean and watch for the cops. If he saw the cops, we would all load up, jump in the plane, take what we can, and leave the truck and the rest of the weed we do not get loaded. We felt pretty safe because even if the cops show up, they probably do not have four-wheel drive and/or do not want to get into a gunfight today. They make very little money probably not enough for gunfighting. We were busy. We unloaded the gas from the plane and poured it into the wing tanks. We then loaded a thousand pounds of weed on the plane and said, "Adios," to Mexico. It was smooth sailing to Site Six in Arizona by Lake Havasu.

After liftoff, I put the plane on its tail, making the steepest climb it could do without stalling, wanting to get way upstairs where the air is like freezing cold. I needed to get my cylinder head exhaust gas and oil temps down so I could push the power levers all the way forward max power cool temps so I could get the hell out of here. I was pretty sure I would not be seeing any other airplanes on this trip until I was closer to the border. There is nothing out here for hundreds of miles, no radar.

I was going to have to descend when I get closer to Tijuana to try and get below the radar. Radar is line of site, the earth is curved, so it's all math—basically not slide rule things. I would start down one hundred miles out and not pull the power, back, and increase speed to redline. I would try and pass 5,000' fifty miles out and 500' twenty miles south of the border.

Flying north, I tried and hugged the mountain ranges that run north-south in that area. It keeps me below the Imperial Valley radar, and the mountains kept me off the San Diego radar. I tried and made it look as if I was going to land in Tijuana. When I got closer, I lined up on a Tijuana runway and slow way down, and on the San Diego radar, it looked as if I was going to land in Tijuana. Before I got within site of the tower, I made a steep bank right turn toward Arizona and poured in as much power as I possibly could while watching the temperature gauges, flying down by the roof tops now working to keep the engine temperatures down. While I tried go as fast as I could, I might have company by some chase planes, but this route might give me some time ahead of any chase planes. This route I might have burned it out by now.

I had sent my ground crew to a place called Site Six. This place was a secret test site for the P-51 Mustang during WWII. It is near Lake Havasue that turned into Lake Havasue City Arizona with a large runway. But the runway I used was the emergency runway for Site Six. It's ten miles northeast of town and separated by a mountain. The strip is two miles long and 200 feet wide.

It's amazing. It's all hard sand and rocks. The grading was done by our military thirty years ago and is just as good as it was during the war. Another reason is that it hardly ever rains out here. When I am landing here, I can see for many miles around the area to see if any sheriffs are around.

The one I put in charge to catch this load was Butch D. He was playing golf in Kingman when I landed. Maybe he was just late for one reason or another. At any rate after I landed, I taxied over to the side of the runway. John and I unloaded the airplane and carried pushed and pulled the bundles of pot to the side of the runway and under the sage brush. There was a lot of sage brush here thankfully.

I asked John if he wanted to wait for Butch and stay with the pot while I flew over to Needles, California, and gassed up. He said whatever I wanted. If Butch doesn't show, it's hard to think someone would miss a $20,000 payday catch fee and a chance to sell as much pot as he could. I was pretty sure he would show some time soon. I needed airplane gas bad, so I jumped over to the Needles Airport. I landed and parked in the fueling area. I tried to park so I could watch the runway for any landing airplanes. After I taxied in and parked so I couldn't get penned in, I walked into the office and put in a fuel order for 200 gallons and paid cash.

The fuel truck was parked in front of my airplane, and the fueler was on top of my plane, pumping in fuel. I was in the cockpit watching the fuel gauges and looking for cops. After a few minutes, a Douglas Skyraider landed. It was painted up like the border patrol cars. He taxied up and parked right in front of me with the fuel truck in the middle. He shut down his giant engine but left on the master switch as I could see over the fuel truck as his rotating beacon on top of his tail is on, and I know his guns are hot. They are electrically charged. (Note to writing room, this would be a good time for an explosion.)

When the fuel truck pulled out from in-between us, I was staring up at the pilot, and I could also see six fifty-caliber machine guns pointing at me. He was looking down at me, and he could see through my front windshield that there were no seats or cargo in my plane; it's empty. I could see his face; we were only about thirty feet apart. He looked pissed off, and he was too late to shoot me down. I won this round.

I started my engines and made a real tight turn. There was just enough room to squeak by our wing tips as they were not the same height this Skyraider is a serious big war plane. It is very heavy. The guns alone weighed thousands of pounds, and so did all the ammo. All that slowed him down thankfully. I was going back to flight training and get my instrument rating, so I could do these things at night.

I took off as soon as I reached the runway—no time for checklist. I would do the checklist later. I had plenty of fuel now. I pointed my plane north headed up to Laughlin, Nevada. My friend had a casino right near to Bullhead City. He had a long grass runway in front of his casino and hotel. I would always have the only twin-engine airplane on his parking area there. Most twin pilots don't like the braking action on grass and only will land on pavement—some insurance bullshit they say.

The parking was by a large glass door that enters into the casino. Sometimes when I landed and parked, a small crowd of people would come out and gather in the patio area with drinks in their hands to see who gets off. They would see the owner come out to meet me and shake hands. The summertime evenings around the Colorado River have no mosquitos and are cool. I built an addition to the school in Bullhead City a few years back, and the owner and I became friends for about a year, while I worked on the school project. He had the best restaurant in town. This is the first time I have been here alone. Usually I would have one or two girls with me or another couple. I walked into the restaurant with my friend, and he usually comped everything. He introduced me to the maître d', and he took me to a table and snapped his finger, and a server came over. I ordered a beer and told the server I would be right back. I had not eaten all day.

Back in the day before they were really popular, the pilots who flew pot were called astronauts. And when I left John in a wildlife refuge full of mountain lions, I knew he was so big and didn't think a mountain lion would mess with him, but

I was concerned for the mountain lions. It was starting to get dark. I called, of course, mission control, and they told me Big John had called in and was on the highway back to my ranch in California.

After I was sure my pot was secured and on the way back to Cali, I decided to kick back gamble and drink and party. I had been working a lot of hours, and I had all the girlfriends here that I needed, and they had rooms down by the Colorado River—one of my favorite playgrounds.

The next morning, I had to fly back to Murrieta hot springs to my ranch and meet up with the ground crew. They should be home tonight to divide up the pot. A few other brothers have joined up. We are in one of the barns. I had a hanging meat scale, and we divided up the smoke. While we were doing this, I was talking to Big John, and he said after I took off from the dirt strip at Site Six, in about ten or fifteen minutes later, a huge round-engine loud airplane flew over the landing strip real low and departed to the south.

I was being chased. He was using some radar tracking that was about ten minutes late. It was maybe good Butch was late; otherwise the pilot would have seen the truck or something and called the sheriff to block the two roads that lead into the area. But nothing was there that he could see. The pot bundles were under the sage brush, and John stayed down. He said after he heard the plane, the intercept pilot must have been fairly surprised when he caught up to me and found that I had unloaded somewhere but not here in Needles.

That next night at the Ranch, we pulled out a chart and started planning the next scam, and it would be at night. This one was to close. Somehow, I always get away anyway.

CHAPTER 2

Growing in Orange County

1953 is when the real lucky fun started happening. This I will never forget. It was in Anaheim, California. In the 1950s no-smog textbook blue skies, you can see the snow all around on the mountains. My favorite mountain was Mount Baldy; I learned to ski there. You could see all the mountains around the Los Angeles basin including where all the passes are to the north and east. The first time I really goofed up was when I tried to coast down Raymond Hill in Fullerton with my Soap Box Derby car that my dad built for me. The grade was almost forty-five degrees, the policeman told my mother. He also said that if the car hadn't rolled over (lucky), I would have been going over one hundred miles an hour at the bottom of the hill where streets cross, with no brakes. All this was happening while I was bleeding and being taken to the hospital in an ambulance.

My brother and his friend helped me push and pull this Soap Box Derby car to another town called Fullerton and up this hill called Raymond. When we finally make it to the top, I asked my brother if he wanted to ride, and he said, "No way."

So I asked his friend if he wanted to ride, and he said, "Sure," and got on. He rolled off just after we started rolling. A few seconds after that, I was going so fast. I just tried to straighten the car out a little bit by turning the steering wheel. A tiny car just snapped, rolled over, and flipped me aside. I had on typical Southern California attire—only shorts, no shirt, no shoes, now no skin.

After my skin grew back, my dad took me out to the garage and took his belt off, and I learned I could jump over cars. But when it was all over with, we had the talk about military school in New York again. Then we got back to normal. And I remembered what my dad said when we finished building the car. He said, "Whatever you do, don't take it up Raymond Hill." I took that as challenge and wanted to prove to him I could do it. I started thinking how I could do it. Everything was fine for a couple years. My dad would take me to the Santa Ana Drag races at the airport. They would shut down a parallel runway to race on Sundays. We would take the back seat and spare tire out of his Cadillac, and he would race it, and he always would win. He had the only overhead valve V8 engine there. We would leave and not take the trophy, and he would tell me not to tell mother the church lady we were racing because she would get mad. The same thing he would say when we went to the horse races. There are a lot of horse races around Los Angeles. I could name all the racetracks in the Los Angeles basin, including Delmar, and how to get there by the time I was ten.

Sometimes I think my father's and my grandfather's lives were more ambitious than mine. My grandfather was an entertainer. He sang and danced, while my grandmother played the piano. They toured around the counties and farmed. He had a yacht we went out on often. My father always had a gun in a holster under his dash panel tied around the steering column. The reason I knew this was that I used to spend a lot of time in his car crawling around in it, waiting for him to come out of a bar. He would say I need a screwdriver to tighten up the loose screws. I know he wasn't a criminal because he would always have a chief of police and/or a captain from the state police and a councilman, mayor, or judge over to his house to play poker on Thursday nights. He would ask me to sit in sometimes when I was much older. I do not think he would ever do anything illegal although I saw him punch a guy once. I was in the car across the street and did not hear anything, but I saw the guy go down like sack of potatoes. My dad just turned around and walked across the street back to the car. He acted like nothing happened and looked normal and smiled and didn't say anything. I don't think I said anything for the rest of the day. When I see an English movie with Vinnie Jones in it, I think of my dad. When my dad and I were horsing around playfully, he would tease me about my lower lip. I have three cuts on it that were stitched up, and the older I get, the easier it is to see them. He would say, "What do you do when you get in a fight? Stick out your lower lip." He was a semi-pro basketball player. He would always take me with him to the games. In those days after the war, most games would end in fist fights, and my dad would be right in the middle of the group—just another Friday night.

The next incident was with my Doodle Bug motor scooter my dad purchased for me. I was riding around Northeast Anaheim on a nice summer weekend day traveling through acres of new home construction sites. There was no traffic or workers, and it was fun until I heard a siren go off. I tried to run, but my Doodle Bug was too low to the ground, and when I cut across some lots, it high centered, and I was thrown off and crashed, and I had a few bruises a little dazed. I could see another officer walking up from the other street. The first officer said he was going to have to give me a ticket for trying to elude the police, and my mother would have to take me to court for this. I was twelve. When my father heard this, he was a little upset and went down to the police station to see the police chief. When he came home, he said some old lady on Liberty Lane called the police because whenever I drove by her house, her dogs started barking. He said, "Just stay away from there, and you will be okay." A couple days later, he purchased a larger Powder Blue Cushman scooter for me. This opened Corona Valley and more places to go. There were no traffic problems in those days.

When I was fourteen, my mother was so nice; she was a pushover. I had an uncle that lived in Carbon Canyon she visited frequently, and I talked her into letting me drive her station wagon around the country roads and that I would stay close. The reason I remember this is that I found a picture with the car and in it, and you can clearly see the new paint on the rear quarter panel. There was a pipe fence around the front of the Carbon Canyon school. I wanted to see how fast the car would go backward, and I didn't because that pipe fence got in the way. I know I am not perfect and do not always do the right thing. It took out the right rear quarter panel, and I do not remember Papa's reaction. When I thought about it, he might have asked her why she would let me drive the car.

I learned how to drive fairly well, and I started pushing my dad's Packard out of the garage late at night with a buddy and joy riding around East Anaheim. On this night, I was planning on going over to—I think—Tommy Murphy's house and spin a doughnut in his front yard. I did a good one with this big car with its big heavy straight eight engine. Incidentally it was my first doughnut. As I left there and came up to the corner, my dad was standing there beside my mother's car. She was with him. They must have watched me do the doughnut. He pretended to be mad and said he would follow me home. It was the military school talk again. This included again, "I have an automatic appointment to the Air Force Academy in Colorado for you because your father was an officer during WWII."

About a couple weeks later, I came home from school, and there was a powder blue 1949 Ford convertible with a white top and white walls but no key. When my father came home from the office, he gave me the keys and told me I could work on the car but not drive it till I get my license. I said, "Don't worry." I replied, "I can wait a little to drive it." I was thinking I couldn't wait till he would leave in the morning. I would drive to school or maybe the beach. I tried to be careful and not drive much, only a few months till fifteen, but it finally happened; I got pulled over by a policeman. I was only fourteen but a little tall for my age. I was on my way to the Been Hut (La Palma drive Inn) for a tostada at lunchtime. I got out of my car and decided to see how fast I could talk. When he walked up, he had a big smile on his face and was very nice. He asked if I knew that a brake light was out. I said no, but I said, "I will fix it today." I told him. I was waiting for him to ask for my drivers. He was just smiling like he was having a good time.

Then he looked deep into my eyes for a moment and leaned forward a little and said, "Maybe you shouldn't be driving around so much." I got the message, so I decided I would not drive to school again till I got my driver's license. After I received my driver's license, I started driving to school, but I could go to the beach. One of the things I did on the weekends was pick up a bottle of Thunderbird wine or a six pack of beer and go to the Orange Drive-Inn movie theater. Going to the beach seemed to happen more and more, and then I got expelled twice for nonattendance. Then we had a ranch address, and I was accepted into the Brea High School. There were no hot chicks, so I only was there for one week, back to the beach. My parents had no control of me after I got my first car—no church. I came and went as I pleased. I usually got home by midnight. My dad didn't care, and my mother was too busy with church to watch over me. This created a big problem because I started going to the beach every day.

Finally, one day, my father who had been wanting to send me to military school for years said, "When you turn seventeen, you are going into the Army!"

I said, "Yes, sir, that is a good plan." There was no war going on, and I had heard Germany has the best beer, and at seventeen, I could drink all I wanted, and I wanted a lot. I was getting into trouble as I see this new '56 Red and White Oldsmobile hardtop with these beautiful Flipper hubcaps near the corner of east street and south street in Anaheim, a low-rent district, and I decided to go back late at night with a buddy and take them for my car. Everything was right. I pulled up in front of the Olds with no lights, and we got out and ran back to the rear tires on each side of the car and popped off the rear hubcaps and started moving up for the front hubcaps, and the car moved little, and some guy was sleeping in the back seat, jumped up, and started yelling in Spanish, so we were already moving to the front of the car, and we just kept moving forward, and we dropped the hubcaps. He was yelling and struggling to get out of the back seat of the two-door car; he was a big man. We piled into my car and sped away, and I was thinking, *Nice car alarm.*

Selling beer along the German Poland border Cold War.

Mom saying goodbye.

Anaheim to the Mexican border is like less than two hours, and sometimes we would drive down there to party and drink beer. We would put the youngest-looking guys in the trunk as there would always be a San Diego policeman at the Mexican port of entry, and the policeman would look inside the car for contraband or juveniles, missing persons, and kidnappings. I don't know, but they did check it out. The last time I went to Mexico to party and learn about sex, we got into a fight in a bar, about the bar bill. All of us were fifteen and sixteen. We fought our way out of the bar and right into a police paddy wagon, waiting for us at the front door then straight to the TJ jail. I was the only one with any money, and the bail was one hundred dollars each. I had the hundred, and I got cut loose and drove back to Anaheim and went to my bank. It was morning by now and drew out enough money to get the other kids out. I didn't think I could go to their parents and tell them I took their kids to TJ to drink and get drunk, and I need a hundred dollars to get them out of jail. They would die in that jail. It was nasty. So I drove back down to TJ, paid their bail money, and never went back there for a few years—only once in the daytime to have my car reupholstered in blue and white tuck and roll. I turned seventeen and was not going to school, so I found myself in a recruiting office, and I signed up for a three-year duty contract, two years in Germany. Before I knew it, I was on a train to Fort Ord, Salinas, California. This would be my first eight weeks of training. I found out that in soldiers' club on the bases, they don't check your ID for age. I guess if you are old enough to get shot, you ought to be able to buy beer. Well I started drinking every day, not enough to mess up my Army career but every day. I think that I knew when to stop. That's why I was not a complete alky at that time. Next was eight weeks of artillery training and then a troop ship to Germany, and this was where connoisseurs of great beer reside. Of course, I had several jobs. The worst was the ammo section—the worst hand loading seventy-five-pound howitzer shells of an on trucks but the best radio telephone operator (RTO) and driver for a forward observer (FO) Lieutenant Sundt. I had to have a security clearance to be a radio telephone operator. My LT was a forward observer. We would drive around the borders of Poland and Germany, looking to see if the Russians have changed their position. At that time, there were no satellites, and we could not do flyovers since they shot down Francis Gary Powers in his U-2 spy plane. One problem was that the borders were not marked very well. When I would be in a small town, I would not like to see soldiers from Poland or Russian walk in. We stopped at a lot of these guesthouses with live ammo. We both loved the Hopps. I was attached to the motor pool and answered only to my LT. The motor pool sergeants would not care when I came in for gas, and I could leave whenever I wanted for my LT. LT told me he did not care what I did with the Jeep. I just had to pick him up at his hotel every morning at eight with a full tank of gas, and if there was a few beers in the trailer, it would be okay. The Germans drink bear with all their meals—what could be a good thing for a person who enjoys the Sudds. I would run around the local guesthouses, buy beer load my trailer and tow it out to where the troops were camped at, and sell it all after dark except what I would drink the next day. I was sent back to the states to a training battalion to finish my three years, and the Vietnam war had started. I got extended for a couple months, which was no big deal. I was on the street again with a vodka problem.

My father was fairly well known in Orange County. He built hundreds of homes and apartments there. When he was in the Army Air Force, he went to a Navigators School in Costa Mesa OC Fair grounds. Several officers liked the area and weather. They all moved to Orange County after the war. They formed the Tigers club in Anaheim. It stands on the corner of Sycamore Street and Los Angeles Street. With two life-size tiger statues guard the giant front doors. Then came Disneyland; Walt was a tiger. Anaheim of all the Orange County towns accelerated so much more than even Santa Ana. They have a National Baseball team, a National Ice Hockey Team, and of course Disneyland. The home sale market was going big time. The orange groves are going down for the level fertile soil. This is perfect for building thousands of new homes. And a thousand people were coming every day to California to buy one.

The Tigers Club had a Sea Scout Base in Newport Beach on the bay. They had a large dock with a sixty-feet all-steel hull with two new big diesel engines. A US Navy retired picket ship was secured to the dock. My father was on the board of directors. He told me when I turned fifteen how to join, and I did it. When I went to the first meeting, I noticed there were several scouts there that I knew from the Anaheim High School swimming and water polo teams. I belonged to both and lettered in swimming and water polo. I held the high school freestyle record for a minute. What I liked about the water polo was when there was a lot of splashing, the refs can't see what's going on. I think I was fifteen now and was driving. I had a ranch address, so I got my license at fifteen. We would sail this boat out to Catalina Island, taking turns on the helm and working out navigation problems, including ADF training. We explored all the inlets around Catalina. There was one little bay we could pull into and drop the hook and spend the night. This cove is too small to be a bay. There is a sunken Chinese junk. All that was left was the ribs and the keel. The ribs were standing up, and it looked like a ship's skeleton. They were cool to dive around. The wildlife was spectacular. There would be hundreds of seals. If you have ever been close enough to a seal to see their teeth, they look like three-inch cat teeth. It would make you not want get to close or try and pet them. They are very fast and beautiful and can be very loud. The west side of Catalina was covered with them. Sometimes most people have never seen it. Avalon Bay has many seals also. This cove was rumored to be a place the Canadians would unload their Canadian whiskey during prohibition. Then it would be brought into Long Beach in smaller boats. This could have been used by marijuana smugglers also. Sometimes, we would sail down to San Diego to the Navy Base. We could tie up there and spend the night and eat in their mess hall. They had the really good food. I found out later when I joined the Army and ate Army food. Things were going really good, something had to happen, and it did.

We went on an overnight date cruise to Catalina. I had my beautiful girlfriend Maryann. I had hidden a six pack of beer in a locker with a pack of Camels. I had smuggled these things aboard for a wildlife night. So someone one told Ross Jones the first mate, and he told Captain Hoag, and after the trip, the captain told me politely that it would be okay if I left the post. He probably drank my beer and smoked my cigs. He was really cool, and he deserved them. Ross Jones turned out to be a state senator because he could not pass the bar.

My father never said anything about me leaving the Sea Scout group. He had to have heard about it. A couple months later, my dad took me to a hockey game in San Diego with the Tigers club on a big bus: the chief of police, the judge, the mayor, councilmen business leaders, and all the usual suspects. The ride down was fairly mellow, but the ride home was a something to see. The boys started drinking on the way down and drank and yelled a lot during the game. Then on the way home, it started to get a little crazy fun. We stopped at a large strip club near the stadium. These guys are drinking, more now dancing in the isle, and getting louder. It's dark in the club, and I was picking up a few drinks and feeling good. I was only fifteen and the only kid. After a while, we loaded up the bus and started heading north. Then it got louder, and there was more drinking and blasting Frank Sinatra and Dean Martin music, no rock and roll. These guys were dancing around and breaking the plastic cups on the floor with mostly empty and unemptied bottles. I was thinking if these guys were trying to impress the kid that got kicked out of the Sea Scouts for drinking. They have done it big time. I had never been invited to any Lions function before, and I was the only kid on the bus. When on the bus, I could walk around and drink what I could or wanted to. I fell asleep or passed out and woke up at home in my bed the next day. A few days later, my dad told me they charged a thousand dollars to clean up the bus after that trip as if he was proud of it or something. I was not sure if my dad was trying to teach me a lesson; if so, what was it?

My father was quite a party guy and car guy. He could really rock a vodka martini. I would never forget the Yellow '53 Buick convertible, with the big gaudy Chrome Waterfall Grill. The overstuffed red leather interior was really soft. He came home with two tan baseball-like hats with sunglasses that folded down from the bill. He called them our converting hats when we were riding with the top down. We would pull the shades down. Of all his cars, he always had a convertible and a couple of sedans in garages or barn somewhere. He gave me several. My first was a '49 Ford convertible. When my brother started driving, he gave him a '63 split-window Corvette. When he started surfing, he gave him a Chevy Nomad. He took very good care of his boys with vehicles. The second car he gave me was a '55 Pontiac two-door sedan. It had a V8 engine that was larger than the Chevrolet engine, and it had three on the tree. This was 1967, and I blew up the 55 engine in a street race, and in 1957, Pontiac came out with a triple carbureted large engine, and I found one out of a wrecked car and put it in my '55 Pontiac. I hung out with some of the Street Sweepers Car Club, but I was only sixteen and I never went to any meetings at Stan Betz's Speed and Paint Shop in downtown Anaheim.

After I came back from Germany, my father sent me to the Army in Oklahoma driving a black '57 Cadillac convertible. Nobody seemed to mind. I was pretty sure it was the only caddy on the base. My next car in the Army was a '58 Ford Deluxe Ranchero. I ended my army career as a supply sergeant and small arms specialist. I was the battery small arms armorer, which means all weapons fifty-caliber MGs on down. I had control and keys for all weapon racks, and sometimes I would take them off base and target shoot or for hunting with an Indian guy built like a horse that I met in a bar. He would know where to go and two hunters in street clothes, jeans and shirt, with US Army M1 Rifles somewhere in Oklahoma out in the boondocks. After we shot the deer, we would bleed them out and take them into the house and then throw them on the kitchen table, and the mom and pop started skinning them out as it happened a lot. I only did it once, and that was enough hunting for me. I only would hunt pheasants after that for a long time, and then there was no more hunting at all for me. I didn't like killing anything that was not poisonous. After the deer hunt, we went to a bar and drank a lot of beer. When I went back to the base, it was early in the morning, and I drove right through the gate with blood in the bed of my truck, waved to the guards, and drove up to my barracks. Everyone was sleeping. I opened the arms room, put the M1s in the gun rack in, and locked them down and any leftover 3030 ammo. But I would always bring them back in good condition. There was no way I would do anything else. It is good I never got caught. It would have been a big Federal offense.

One time, I went to the warehouses to pick up some weapon, cleaning things, and material with the motor pool driver and noticed nobody was checking anything, and there were a few civilian trucks parked backed in there. I have been waiting for delivery of these things for a while. My mind was grinding because everybody in my battery or company needed something, and this warehouse had everything wall to wall. So I was thinking about stealing from the Army and giving it back to the Army—could it be legal? I was supply sergeant. All these people were asking me for these different things, and I could not get them, or it took forever. But I could get them because I know where they were and I had a truck. If I can't find anything, I can just ask somebody on the loading dock with my sergeant stripes. Soon everyone in my battery had all things they needed, and I was popular. The company captain even said hi to me once after I saluted him. I had a couple privates that worked for me, and we would go to the loading docks and walk around and load up anything we wanted. I always thought if I never took anything out of the gate, this would always be okay, and it was. I was a teenage noncommissioned officer (NCO), so I had my own room and could come and go as I pleased. My drinking was becoming a big problem. Somehow, I met this cook who was drinking vodka all day long every day. He knew all the bootleggers in town. In Oklahoma, you could not buy booze on holidays and Sundays and at night sometimes. I had a nice room, but I could not bring in any women into it, and that was the problem. I did, and the barracks manager found out I had a woman in my room and started banging on the door, and I jumped out the window. I could have been drinking. It was late in the night, and I forgot I guess that I was on the second story, and luckily, I landed on my head and had only a minor concussion with a big melon on the side of my head. I found out the next day in the hospital. I think because I was such a good supply sergeant and spent time in the hospital with much pain, they thought I had suffered enough and forgot about it. It was not long after this incident I was discharged from the Army to Anaheim with an honorable discharge.

After I was discharged out of the Army, I wanted to be a pilot, and I was going to reenlist and be a helicopter pilot. The problem I had was that I was too young to go to Officer Candidate School. You must be twenty-one, I was only twenty. I would turn twenty-one in six months. However, I seemed to be having a wonderful life. I started thinking maybe I had enough of all the military life. I did not like helicopters that much anyway. And later I would use my GI bill to pay part of my flight training years later. I made several trips to Mexico using it to pay for the aircraft rental.

CHAPTER 3

Living in North County

I moved into one of Papa's apartment complexes. It was a hundred units by Katella Blvd and Haster Streets, close to Disneyland in Anaheim. I had a good friend that was the sales manager at Guaranty Chevrolet in Santa Ana, and he gave me a sales job at night while I was going to Fullerton Junior College.

Paul's Supper Club on Garden Grove Boulevard was the best hookup place. Bobby Hatfield (Hats) and his band played there on the weekends, and sometimes he would stop the music when I came in the door and wave and say hi. He always called me Bobbie's little brother, referring to my sister who was in his class and student government with Bob Hatfield. They were two years older than me. I would be going to the nightclub after working at the Chevy store and have nice clothes on short hair and drove a new Chevrolet demo car from the dealership. At least I looked like someone important. This was 1962–1963, and also, I would run into some of my Anaheim buddies in the club. There one was Joel Hoare. I would go with him to play pool on the Anaheim Strip across from Disneyland. There were large hotels with nightclubs bars and pool tables with money. I was pretty buffed up after recently been in the Army for three years. Joel always won! All of this went on for a good while, and then, my father moved to Escondido because land was cheaper and there was more of it. It would make him a larger profit margin. Also it was closer to La Costa. He asked me to move down there and go to work for him and manage some projects. It was a good offer, and I wanted to work outside. I took him up on it and had worked for some of his contractors while going to high school, and I could handle a hammer and carpenter tools.

I moved down to North San Diego County and started construction work for my dad and was very busy. Then I received a call from the Fullerton police, and they said that I could come to work for them as I had applied about a year earlier for a job. I had passed all the test and interviews, which surprised me as I had had incidents with the Fullerton police before and they knew my name. I called and turned it down because I was making twice as much money, and I had financial obligations that cost more than a policeman makes. I must have been at the bottom of their list, or the list was alphabetical. I started framing with one of my father's crews and picked it up real fast. I started doing layout and the more difficult things and formed a framing company after a couple years. I was framing all the houses for my dad and few other builders around North San Diego County. I was hugely successful. I was hugely successful by the time I was twenty-six. I had my own home with a swimming pool. I had a super long telephone wire, so I could sit in my pool and make all my contractor calls after work with a beer. Now that was a status thing with me. I had a silver Corvette, several trucks, and an Indian flathead motorcycle. I owe a lot to my dad. He would not have done the things—he did not loan me a million dollars—but he took me to meet the president of the savings and loan that could loan me money to build speculation homes. That could be more than a million dollars. One of the best things he gave me was an American Express card with no limit. He said to just pay him every month, and this was always in cash. I purchased several yachts and airplanes with it, as well as many charters. Later when I had my tax evasion trials, I always wondered and was glad they never brought Dad in. I don't think they wanted to mess with him. He was a guy that would get more into you than your face. They did get one of his Cadillac dealers and Harley dealer in to testify at my trial. I purchased a new Cadillac Eldorado and a Bonanza airplane with a stack of cash. When I passed him in the courtroom hall, during the trial, he said why I didn't just tell me. I was thinking, Tell him what! That the money was under the table. Well I didn't know there was a difference, but I guess this is what they call the Wild West. Father helped me a lot, but I was a real hard worker, and that is all he wanted to see. I was a heavy drinker after the Army, and he drank a fair amount also, but we always got up to meet for breakfast before going to the jobs. When the San Diego Chargers did their training in Escondido behind the Holiday Inn, my father knew the owner of the Holiday Inn, Tommy somebody. He would have breakfast with Tommy and Sid Gillman every morning while the football team was in training in town. I built a lot of houses and helped him build many houses and apartments. Several carpenters worked for me, and we all became good friends.

Prior to this date, the only drugs I knew were alcohol and tobacco, and I had them down pretty good. Alcohol only got me in trouble one time. I wanted to be an airline pilot, and a DUI would wreck it. That's probably why I led the police through a two-county chase ending in my driveway hidden to the street because of my avocado grove. I did not think they would follow me up my winding driveway. Wrong they did and gently helped me out of my car into theirs. They almost had to carry me. I was not going to blow. That was one thing my dad told me that I remembered, and later I was super glad I remembered. My dad told me if I blow, I could not be helped, and I would have no chance in court. After I was released from San Diego County Jail the next morning, they never took my driver's license. I knew they would take my license at some point, so the next day, I flew my bonanza over to Albuquerque and stopped at a motel and picked up a business card with their address on it and then drove over to driver's license office. I filled out an application, and after paying $35.00, I had a nice New Mexico photo driver's license. They never did ask me to surrender my California driver's license. The next day, I drove over to George Chula's office and talked to George who was a close friend of mine. I told him that I could not have this put on my record at any cost. He knew about my airline ambitions and understood about no chance for me to ever be an airline pilot with a DUI on my record. He said that the trial was in San Diego, so he would have to make a few calls and to call him the next day. The next day, I called, and he said twenty-five, The next day, an aluminum briefcase was delivered to George's office with $25,000 in twenties. I love to get rid of some of these twenties. I have a truck full I call them evidence. When I started this endeavor, we had $500 and $1,000 bills, which made it easy to carry $25,000. One of Reagan's ideas to stop drug dealers was to make no more $500 and $1,000 bills. It did make us carry heavier loads both ways. Meanwhile George put one of his lawyers on my case, James. He got the charges dropped to reckless driving. Jim proved to the court that I could have not been drunk if I led the police on an over early morning fifty-mile trip at over one hundred miles an hour. I was driving my new 1972 suicide four-door Thunderbird. I never had to go to court over this. I wonder what the cops who arrested me thought about all this. I was working on several framing jobs at the same time. This one job I had ready to turn over to the inspectors and dry-wallers is important because I would get a $10,000 draw from the bank, and I only owed my workers a few thousand. I needed to go over there and check all the pickup work—the things like backing for the drywall, a platform for the heater to sit on, and all the corners straight and so on. There was always something to do, and it's better to get it done now than later when you would have to work around people.

I took one of my best and favorite carpenters with me to help finish up. I decided to take a break, and we sat down. I smoked Marlboros like a train. Dan (RIP) was young and very bright. I think he got some Palomar College time, and like me, we thought we knew more than the teachers. For his age, he knew all about carpenter work and mechanical work. He could do all the task necessary to build a house without supervision or take an engine out of a car or truck, rebuild it, and put it back better than new. As I lit up my cigarette, he pulled out a joint and asked for my lighter and lit the joint. I was twenty-five years old and had never seen a joint before. Dan asked if I would like to try this, and I had seen things were changing about the perception of weed and smoking it. It is fun they say, so why not try it. And I did. After much smoking and laughter, we finished up the job, picked up our tools, and drove over to the beach. Needless to say, over the next few months, I was able to stop smoking tobacco, and my drinking slowed way down. When you do construction work, I don't care how old you are or what kind of shape you are in, you would hurt some every day after work, and a joint seems to make it all go away. And it does it without a hangover. After a while at the beach, we drove back to Escondido and went to the Dug-Out, a seedy dive bar in Escondido where a lot of construction workers meet after five to hit on the bartenders. We drank a few beers there, and we each went home. I felt really good the next day after the smoke. The only thing I could think about was how nice the day was, which usually is in Escondido, California, and it seemed a little nicer. I had plenty to do that day, and I did not have much time to think about the smoke. I don't think I saw Dan for a few days. Then at the end of the week, we wound up together at the Dug-Out bar. After a few beers, we decided to go over to a friend's steakhouse Grouper on Valley Boulevard in Escondido. We ate steaks and drank beer till late and then went back to my house for some smoke. Again it turned out to be a nice evening, and I asked Dan how I might obtain some of these herbs. He told me one of my carpenters had some for sale. So this was all going on under my nose for several years, and I knew nothing about it. These herbs have cut my alcohol use by at least 75 percent and got me off smoking tobacco. I was sure this weed could get everybody off opioids. If marijuana was easily available, Medicine without Borders was started by me. They were putting people in jail for even small amounts of it. I never wanted to get higher than one big joint, and a couple beers would take me. Weed was harder to obtain than heroin, and that is what is killing everyone—opioids or addicting them—so they would steal or kill to obtain some. The big money does not want to recognize marijuana as a good drug to use for physical or mental problems. They want to get everybody addicted to their opioids so they can make more money. The problem is that there are so many overdoses. The states that have modern-day hemp laws have less overdoses and problems from opioids.

Everything was fine for a while. I was starting to get into the weed life and enjoying just doing it for recreation and not doing it before or during work; that would be a downfall. It went well with a couple beers after work or on weekends. I wasn't thinking about it until a couple guys I got to know, now that I was a smoker of herbs. One day, Ray, who worked for me, and Carl, who was a friend who has come to some of my parties said they had a kilo of weed and wanted to know if they could keep at my house until they sell it as they both lived with their parents and didn't want to keep it in their houses until they could sell it. They were both first-year college students. They were afraid if their parents found it, they might throw it away or call the police or something, and they said they would give me an ounce for keeping it, and I had never seen a full ounce let alone a whole kilo. I always never had any quantity of any drug on me that I could not eat, so I could not ever have a chance of a drug offense. I should have worried a little more about my taxes. It only lasted a couple days. The kids were running around the house with hands full of cash. When it was all gone, they left and on their way to rent an apartment. Ray, I lost track of, but Carl you could say I knew him until he died on a horse ranch in Fallbrook, California. Carl (RIP) would be mentioned a few times through several decades.

I was thinking that selling weed is a lot easier than building houses and a lot more money can be had. I think with that song came out, "Money for nothing and chicks for free," that sound I liked. It took me about fifty years to figure out that chicks are never free. I could see that song lyrics could be said about smuggling and selling large amounts of weed could relate to that song. I liked being infamous and bringing Timothy Leary to the ranch. It was not my idea, and I had nothing to say about it. I was sure I helped pay for it from weed sales at the time. I liked Tim but not all his things like I don't want anybody to drop out; I want them to lead in the peace and love movement. Rojo told me I could go to the Idyllwild ranch anytime I want, and I could live there if I wanted to. The first time I went, I took my bolt cutters and cut a lock and put my own padlock on the lock chain around gate. Any California rancher knows about that. I would go up there sometimes to take my sheep dog up there to play with JD's (RIP) sheep dog and smoke some good hash and whatever drug was going on at the time. But I had my own ranch, and my wife (RIP) at the time grew up on a ranch and liked the beach and the two Country Clubs close shopping; she was pretty much done with ranches. However, she did go up there with me several times. When hash loads came in, there would be parties up there and sometimes in Santa Cruz. I got busted in Laguna Beach, or I should say the front door got busted when Romain and Purcell broke the door down and raided the house I was at. One of those two cops busted Tim. On this bust, Tad flushed the small amount coke we had, and they found a little weed and took all six of us to jail. I have George Chula's home phone number, and I called him. He drove down to Laguna and picked us up in his avocado green Cadillac, and no charges or record of this was ever saved. The chick I was with told me on the way to her house never to call her again! I think she was in shock for the whole ordeal in jail. Out of jail, she was from back east somewhere, not used to the Wild West legal system in Calie. George had a Christmas party, and when I arrived, I had been drinking, and I could not find a parking spot. So I parked in his front yard with my new Thunderbird. I did not know that officers Purcell and Romain were also invited to the party. These guys were all a bunch of crooks. Anyway, on the drive to drop off the others in Laguna from the Laguna Police Station, after we dropped the others off, George drove me over to my townhouse by the Santa Ana Airport and told me about those two cops being at his party along with other cops and judges' lawyers. One of the judges was a friend of my dad's. When we crossed paths in George's house, he asked me why I was there.

I said, "Free booze." He just smiled. George said that the Laguna cops saw my car in his front yard at the party. He said they saw it again parked in front of a house they were watching in Laguna and thought they hit a jackpot. The house belonged to a brother (RIP) who was in Hawaii at the time. I told George they would never see me in Laguna again. I have never been back. I can survive fine. The brothers would come to me after this.

The first time I drove up to see Tim was after Rojo told me I should go up there and meet him. On the way, I passed three G cars with two men in them each with ties on. The dirt road up to the ranch was only a few miles long, and three G cars in that short of distance were bad news. I know they got my license number. I was driving a car that looked like a G car late-model four-door sedan in gold color. I had leased it for transportation to my boat factory in San Luis Rio, Colorado. The car was in my name also, and that's what started the tax evasion charges, I think. They could not ever catch me in the act of smuggling or with a large stash. On the top of the mountain behind the ranch where the teepees are at, you could see palm springs, the mountains, the Beaumont Banning Pass, and about a hundred miles of desert and mountains. It is a simply unbelievable view. Seeing a sunrise from here would be enlightening to say the least. This is an everyday event for a pilot, but I can see it would be an exceptional awaking and moving sight for a ground pounder.

I was buying weed from a few dealers in North San Diego County and driving it up to Orange County and selling it to people that were friends I went to school with in Anaheim, Lincoln Fremont, and Anaheim Union High schools. This brought in a little extra cash, and I could smoke for free. But I wanted more money, and it worked out for me because I got a job, building twenty-five houses in Chula Vista, a town between San Diego and Tijuana Mexico. The contractor that started the project had a gambling problem and went broke. He let the subdivision run down, and Silvergate Savings and Loan repossessed it. They gave me the job to finish building out the project. I had my foreman running the construction work up above with the houses. The road down below was a third of a mile of a steep grade. It was like forty-five degrees too steep for any machines. This would have to be all hand work, replanting the ice plant to stop erosion, and it had largely flooded out due a wet year and a poor landscaping design. The rain started rushing down the steep hill and washing out the ice plant. I needed to build some concrete shoots in a few low areas to handle most of the water to drain down and level all the ground to replant all the washed-out ice plant. If you do construction work in Southern California, you would pick up enough Spanish to get by and run a crew. Usually one or two Mexicans would speak a little English, and that helps. I know the border fairly well as I have gone down to Mexico and purchased much Mexican floor bathroom and kitchen tiles. Some of the best things I brought back to use in my houses was beautiful hand-carved front doors. I wanted to bring back weed but did not want to do it under their noses. The border is very large, and the Pacific is the largest ocean. I knew where to pick up the farm and construction workers at San Ysidro, a town on the border. I hung around there for a while and hired ten men at $10 an hour and one with an old 1951 Ford pickup truck and red hair and freckles. His name was John for $15 an hour and was a really cool dude I could tell. We did some things. His father was wealthy and had a home in downtown TJ with big iron doors and a twelve-foot wall around it. I told the men I had hired to get on John's truck and follow me out to the job that was only a couple miles away. My truck was loaded with pioneer tools, picks, shovels, and carpenter tools for the concrete forms. I charged the bank $30 an hour per man. The bank gave me all my draws in cash because I was using a lot of Mexican workers and had to pay them in cash every day. One day, John asked me if I wanted to see his truck motor. All the men were working on the hill as we were walking toward his truck. He was telling me that when he changed his truck over to twelve volts, he moved the battery to the engine compartment. He opened the passenger door and pulled the rubber floor mat up. There was a compartment for the six-volt battery. He told me he could put two kilos of pot in it and would do it every day five days a week. I was in shock for only a moment, but he had been working for me a couple weeks, and I think he just wanted to get to know me before he brought this up. Of course, I was very happy as I was taking up weed to Orange County on the weekends, sometimes to the city that we called San Francisco. I was selling it to most of my Anaheim High School friends and fronting some to Rosey, Rojo's wife. She told me the brothers purchased a sailboat and did not leave enough money for the length of their trip, and if not for me, they would not have any food money. She said the wives were selling small amounts of weed at the Taco Bell. I was happy to do this as I sold a lot of weed to the guys and the girls were very nice.

Around this time, Orange sunshine LSD was the newest thing going around. I asked one of my friends about it. They said that it was the brotherhood in Laguna that had control of it. The leader you know we went to school with him and some of the members. I had no idea I would be running with these guys for the next two decades. He told me who they were and said, "They have a store in Laguna. I will take you over there now. If you want to go, you can buy all the LSD you want, and it is the best. No bad trips ever and colors to blow your mind with no hangover."

I said, "Let's go." I had just picked up a wad of cash. It was good timing because everybody was talking about it, and I could sell a lot. I don't think anybody had it in San Diego. I was pretty sure there was none in Mexico yet. and it was probably legal there. We drove to the store in Laguna. The store was just opened. Everything was all new and very nice. We arrived there. We went into the back of the store and into a nice-size room with no chairs and no furniture, and I talked to a brother. I remembered him from Anaheim High School. We touched base a little, and then he told me to go to the trailer park north of town on Laguna Canyon Road. I was driving my silver Corvette. I thought it might stick out there but so what. I followed their direction and pulled up beside an old silver small trailer, and there was a fat man in it. His name was Skinny. I purchased 500 little Orange barrels. There was no need to count them. I quickly found out if you count very many, it's just like taking them. They fit in to a small baggy about the size of a D cell battery. They had called him from the store and told him I was coming and that I have been selling weed in Anaheim and had connections in Mexico and had some to sell and could get much more. We talked about me selling weed to them.

Skinny told me, "Go to dodge city and meet Rojo and a telephone number. He will buy all the weed you have or can get if you front it to him." I was thinking Brotherhood of love, with kids from Anaheim that I knew from grade school. What could go wrong. He was very happy. When I left, he called me brother. We did not know we would be moving tons of weed in next few years, and I would come in contact with the tabbing machine that pressed out the pills. It was in desert's house near Bermuda Dunes, south of Palm Springs many years later. I sold them most of the weed I smuggled into Arizona from Mexico. I sold them a few thousand pounds of pot. Then when Arizona was burned out, we moved to Texas. I fronted tons of weed to them, and they always paid until I met a brother; they called him Kilo John.

I wanted to go into the interior of Mexico in the jungle where the great weed is grown. My lime green Guadalajara was very good, but some dealers were getting bigger and better buds.

Chapter 4

Searching for PV

I had been working a couple years with my brothers in Anaheim and Laguna Beach selling weed. I found a very large demand for weed, a lot larger than I could supply with my Tijuana connections. My brothers from Laguna explained to me they could easily sell all the pot I could bring into this country. I had been very successful with my construction company and had made a lot of money selling smaller amounts of weed. I had a lot of green cash because I was getting all my bank draws in cash. I was in very good with a San Diego bank that my family was using. I had told the bank that most of my workers were from Mexico, and I needed cash to pay them with. Sometimes I would pick up over $10,000 a week in cash, sometimes more. I wasn't paying my income taxes, so my cash was building up very fast. I had enough green cash to buy tons of weed in Mexico and ship it to the USA.

There was only one thing for me to do—to get away from the border weed trash. I wanted to go to the interior of Mexico where weed is cheap and could be excellent. I wanted to buy tons and find a way to bring it into the country. My company owned pickups and Corvettes, but I needed something better for my long trip into Mexico, and I had planned to spend at least two months there. I was hoping I could find the best pot and people that were successful to deal with in that time frame.

People who are already successful generally have more to lose and are more careful on their movements. I had the cash, and a deal should come together, before two months is up. The main thing that would take the time was that I wouldn't work with the first opportunity and wanted to find somebody that was rich and/or well to do. That would be able to keep us out of jail, not go to jail, so no rush. I decided to build the best vehicle for the job. It was decided a Jeep four-wheel drive pickup. This Jeep would get me to the beach, mountains, and jungle. I replaced the Chevy six cylinder with a Chevy V8 and had it painted white. Put on large wide white wheels and aggressive tires. I purchased a new cab-over camper. It was fully equipped with everything, so we could sleep in if we had to. I planned on staying in nice hotels most of the nights. I built a special compartment behind the seat in the cab and a couple compartments inside the camper. You needed a tool to enter them.

It was 1967, and Mexico was like the wild Wild West. My traveling partner was Delmar Johnson. He is a friend I met in San Diego at one of my parties. We got to know each other fairly well. He was built like a football linemen and buffed. He looked like James Gandolfini although a whole lot younger. I was like a quarterback not quite as buffed, but if you drive nails all day long with a twenty-eight-ounce waffle head hammer, for several years, anyone would have a fair amount of mussel aboard. We both had hot chicks for girlfriends, and we did really good with all the other ladies.

We would never intentionally hurt anyone, but we would not look like we would be a pushover for bandidos or the Federales. Having been in jail in Tijuana during my teen years, I knew a little Spanish and had lots of Mexican workers and growing up in Southern California. I had to learn a little Spanish, although I knew the Spanish numbers fairly well. I understood about the Mexican legal system. Just pay them, and you are free no record. It was not really much different than the USA but easier to do in Mexico. I thought the laws would be a little slacker the deeper we went into Mexico.

I had heard about Puerto Vallarta and wanted to go there. It was a small fishing village at the time. There was a movie filmed there many years ago. Cobblestone streets were very quaint, and the closest city is Guadalajara. It's connected by this dangerous mountain twisty road from Tepic to Puerto Viarta with a lot of blind curves. It has a cliff on one side of the road and no guard rails, like hundreds of feet drop off. When it rains a lot, they have a few of tour buses crash there every year. But it has beautiful scenery. I have driven it many times, but they do have several flights a day to Guadalajara. That's what I like.

Delmar and I left for Mexico. The first stop would be San Ysidro border station. We drove by the San Diego police posted at the border to look into your car and truck and see if you look old enough. Then we drove a few feet, and we were in Mexico and stopped at the Aduana Station. We told them we were going to Mazatlán and then on to Puerto Viarta. They told me to pull over, and one of the Aduanas came over and we got out. He looked inside the cab and the camper and did not find my stash of money pot, hash, crystal mescaline, and sunshine. That was two months' supply and it's a good thing I had built the secret compartments, or we might have not got very far into Mexico.

After the search, they directed us to the Mexican Visa building. They went over my truck registration and insurance papers. Everything checked out, so a little cash changed hands, and we had visas and stickers for our windshield. While we were in the office, we noticed two hot little chicks checking us out a little, as we were checking them out. We seemed to all walk out together.

The older one Jenifer said she and her sister lived in Guadalajara and had to come to San Diego to do some shopping and renew their visas. They were on the way to the airport and overheard that we were heading south and wanted to know if they could they ride along. First, I thought this was a sign of a good trip and looked up into the sky and said to myself, "Thank you."

We told them we were going to Mazatlan, spend a few days on the beach, and then go on to Puerto Viarta. We did not have any plans past that. They said that was perfect. They could ride with us to Puerto Viarta and fly on to Guadalajara when we arrived in Puerto Vallarta.

They were like college-age girls and seemed very educated and fun, so I told them I had a whole bunch of stash so the trip would be fantastic. That Jeep had heavy duty shocks on it, but it was like rocking and knocking all the way to Mazatlan. It could cruse eighty all day long and didn't seem to mind the bumps on the bad Mexican roads. I would drive for a while, and Delmar and Kate would sleep in the camper. Then Delmar would drive, and Jenifer and I would be resting and sleeping in the camper. This way, we could drive straight through. We made a few stops on the way for food and beer and tequila.

Clubbing in Mexico

I have no idea how many days it took us to reach Mazatlan, not many, but we partied all the way. These girls completely drained us of all our energy, and I was glad to see the beach and think about getting some sleep for a change. When we pulled into town, we drove directly to the beach area. We found a nice campground on the beach in around some nice hotels. We backed into our camping spot and kicked back. We sent the girls out to find some beer and food, and we took naps. I learned that this was not the first time these girls had renewed their visas in San Diego. We only stayed in Mazatlan for three days.

While we were there on the beach, Richard walked right through our campground with a woman. He was about two feet from me and looked right at me and said, "Hello."

I was in a little shock and said, "Hello," back as they passed us. He probably could see us from his hotel room and went out of his way to pass us and see us up close. I was thinking what would have happened if I would have asked him if he wanted a smoke and some sunshine, but there was no telling where that would go. At the time, Richard was the funniest of all comedians. He had me almost crying before from laughing so much. I think he set his self on fire, and that makes me think maybe that's why I did not ask him to have a smoke. I do not like fire. It is the worst malfunction ever for in airplane.

We played on the beach with the girls. Then we walked down the beach and rented a Hobie Cat. We sailed out around the uninhabited offshore islands. We were passing one, and we could see a guy and girl in swimsuits franticly waving their arms. So I spun around and landed on the beach. They walked over and told me they swam out in the morning and tried to swim back but couldn't make it. They decided it was easier to come back to this island. Evidently, they did not know about the tide.

They asked if they could ride back with us, and I couldn't leave them there. So we shoved the Hobie Cat out to about four feet of water, and all climbed aboard. This Cat was not designed for six passengers. The whole Cat sunk about twelve inches below the surface, but it floated with all of us, and it was fairly windy, and we sailed back to shore slowly. It must have looked funny six people sailing. and they could only see the mast and a sail. The next day I rented the Hobie Cat again, and we sailed around for a while. It was pretty windy, so I unloaded everybody, and I wanted to Surf with the Cat.

I was feeling pretty good, and I traveled down the beach a little ways where the waves were longer and larger. It was easy with an onshore wind. I could sail up on the top of the wave with one sponson, and the wind and the sail would hold up the other sponson. I made I couple passes in front of some hotels, and I noticed a person running down the beach waving and yelling at me to come in. I pulled into the beach, and it was the guy I rented the Hobie Cat from. He was real pissed and told me to get off the boat, and I could never rent it again.

No more Hobie Cat, so it's time to leave Mazatlán. There was one more thing to do: to ride the parachute pulled by a boat ride. It was a cool ride. We could see so much, and the ride seemed really smooth. You could feel much the air was so clear here, nothing like California.

We loaded everything up and departed the campground for Puerto Viarta. My truck was single cab, so we would take turns driving. We could pull over anywhere and rest or spend the night along the road. Again, I do not remember how many days it took us to get to PV. That's what the cool kids call it. We wanted to get the sisters' home, so we went by the airport on the way into town. I wanted to get tickets for the sisters. It was a short flight. Jenifer told me that she and her sister told their parents they were staying at a girlfriend's house in San Diego for a few days. Jenifer said their dad would send a car for them. I asked her if the driver would notice what plane they get off of. She said he would notice whatever I told him.

The next flight to Guadalajara was the next day. The only thing to do was check into a nice hotel with two rooms on the beach. We all took showers, not together. I was running out of skin, and then we dressed up and went out clubbing. This would be a wild sendoff night. They really wanted to be remembered. I wanted to remember Jenifer because I just knew I was destined to go to Guadalajara. We dropped the girls of at the Puerto Vallarta airport. This meant we would finally get some sleep. These two little sweeties ate our lunch. I knew I would hook up with them again. They were very fine nice young ladies with manners and everything else. All this made me like Mexico all that much more.

We parked the truck and went into the terminal. We wanted to make sure the sisters got on the right plane. We were all a little tipsy early in the day. After we kissed them goodbye, we drove around town a little looking for a two-bedroom house or condo on the beach that I could rent for a couple weeks or so. I really liked it here. I really wanted to get into the jungle and mountains though because that's where the tons were cheap.

I love the cobblestone streets and beautiful open-air restaurants with fine food and fresh fish, like the old wood fishing boats were right by the restaurants. There were no transportation charges. We were only a couple hours away from home by jet airliner, not halfway around the world. This is why several actors have homes here. We found a better hotel and rented a two-bedroom bungalow that was right on the beach. We could leave the sliding door open at night, then see and hear the surf, and smell the sea.

We rested a couple days and stayed at the hotel and used their beach, no driving. They had a nice restaurant and bar.

We started to go out to the nightclubs—not that many in town including the one in our hotel. The best one turned out to be rumored to be owned by Frank Sinatra. It was called El Bandido, and it had live music and a good crowd. It was next door to a small strip mall. I thought that if we started hanging around the clubs, we might make a few friends and run into someone we could trust enough to buy weed from—not just some guy hanging around the club but someone that owns a business or something to show for his existence. The other possibility would be to go to Guadalajara. The sisters went to the American school in Guadalajara. They said they know Mexican rich kids that went to the American school. Some of them were related to the underworld there. It's crazy.

The nightclub we ended up at night the most was the El Bandito. It was very popular and was on the outskirts of town southside. The club was connected to a small strip mall. You could call us regulars after a while. We got to know all the servers and bartenders. I was a rich contractor looking to buy a home in Viarta. This is a tourist town, and population changes every week. We finally got to meet the manager of the bandido one night, Dr. David Ortiz. He came down and joined us for a drink. I was sure he was told we have been spending mucho dinero and were good guys. We had started meeting Dr. David several nights and taking turns buying drinks for each other. I told him I was looking for a summer home in Viarta.

Dr. David recommended Casa Palomar, he said he knew the people who owned it and said we could probably rent it and even buy it if I wanted. He said it was the house that Richard Burton and Ava Gardner lived in when they shot the movie *Night of the Iguana.* It is a beautiful house on top of a hill that is on the approach to the Puerto Vallarta airport. You can look out the front bay window and see you were lined up with the runway and looking right down the runway, as if you were on a low final approach. It got a little noisy. The Airplanes go right over the top of us. It looked like they were at least a thousand feet high or higher. Inside the house was like a garden. There were several geckos with little suction cups for feet. They played on the walls.

The house was divided into two sections with the kitchen in the middle. The house was all white. It had unbelievable tile work and more gardens. It had a large circler driveway in front, with a huge motorhome-size garage in the back. It was great for my truck. It would fit in a corner of it. There was a cleaning lady that came in the morning if we wanted. She would wash all our laundry. There also was a gardener that came once a day to take care of the flowers. We never did see him much, but the gardens were immaculate with nice colorful flowers every day. I felt pretty good about renting it; how many people have slept in a bed Richard Burton slept in.

Dr. David and I became close friends. He even visited me on my estate in Green Valley, California, a couple times. We never talked about drugs, only other things. I did not want him to know about my other operations smuggling. Maybe he figured it out, but who cares. I owned a construction company, so it all was and looked legal.

Next to the El Bandido was a clothing store, and we stopped in there on the way to eat dinner at the club one evening. I could see the front of the store. It looked really nice, and I wanted to pick up some local beachwear. We walked in and noticed that this was a designer's store. The owner came out to the front and introduced himself as Ricardo, a clothing designer. His partner came out from the back, Paulo, and we shook hands. I could tell these guys were gay and probably got high. They were not flaming but just really nice guys. I knew we had struck gold. These guys would be able to help me find weed. Delmar and I bought swimming suits, shorts, long pants, and shirts with Nero collars. They all looked really good. The clothes were all made of super soft cotton and very comfortable around the beaches. I spent a few hundred dollars the first time. These guys were giddy with all the money I just gave them.

I invited them to come over to Casa Palomar. They knew where it was at. We smoked and drank for a while. Then I asked them if they had ever done sunshine acid. They said they had heard about it but had never seen any. I had been checking them out for a few days, and they seemed to be of sound minds. I thought they would be able to safely use sunshine. I liked to be careful who I gave it to—someone who is mental. It should only be subscribed by doctors. It was legal in Mexico. They had not caught up yet. They invited us to go to Mizmaloya with them the next Sunday.

I gave them each a couple hits and warned them to be careful when they take it. We called it a night, and they climbed into their Benz convertible and drove down the hill. We went back to their store the next day. They didn't open until noon. I could not believe their eyes were so wide open. They were so nice to us.

This would be the perfect time for me to ask them if they could score some pot for us. I told them that I had room to take fifty kilos back with me to the states. They said they could do it, but it might take a while though. I said, "Fine. Let me know when you find it." I was at this point when I was not worried about the police, and I was completely not worried about us being turned into the police because when those guys dropped that acid, they went home and went to places they never even contemplated could be real. And I could tell their little world was turned around just by looking in their eyes. Sunshine is amazing, but for most people, once or twice is enough. It was legal in Mexico at the time, but I was sure if you got caught with any weight, they would treat it like cocaine or heroin, until they figure it out, which could take several years while you were in jail. The last time I flew commercial into Guadalajara. Mexico. Their Aduana took me into the back room of customs area and searched me but did not look inside my cassette tape stereo player. They would have me because there was five hundred little orange barrels in the battery case. After taking the sunshine, they seemed to have a little more respect for us, and I told Ricardo and Paulo that I would give them more when we leave.

A few days passed, and I went back to pick up my clothes that I had purchased and Ricardo altered for me. They told me that they had made contact with the farmers and would have the weight in about a week. I could tell these guys were not dealers, but I enjoyed working with them and felt safe. I was not sure about what the kilos would look like.

Since we were going to be here for a while, waiting for the stash, I decided I would fly up to Guadalajara for a few days and visit Jenifer. I wore all of Ricardo's clothes up there, and I probably looked like some kind of crazy beach bum. I was defiantly cool and comfortable. I rented a car and drove out to the Ranchoes, a large gated and walled community with armed guards on the outskirts of Guadalajara. After identifying myself and driving through the gate, a body search, and a phone call, I picked up Jenifer at this Palacio Estate. It turned out her father was an accountant and an executive for a large oil company in Texas and retired. This guy must have had a humongous golden parachute. He liked it here and started building houses to make much more money. Guadalajara is a lot closer to Texas than California. We went out to dinner. There were dark drive-in restaurants in Guadalajara. They called them make-out drive-in's pretty cool. It had very poor lighting, and cars were separated by large plants. We ate there and made out, then went to Mariachi square to listen to the music, dance, and drink cervezas and then cocktails.

On the way back to her home, she told me that her father had invited me to dinner at their house the next night. She had told her father that I was a contractor in California and on vacation. I thought my interest in construction would give us plenty to talk about rather than how we hooked up. When I decided to fly up to Guadalajara, I took a couple days' worth of clothes, and they were all Alfonso's beach clothes.

Jenifer answered the door after the chimes welcomed me. They probably thought I was some kind of a beach bum hippie sitting here with this family, the two sisters having a good time with me. We cooked up a story of how we met.

The dad was really nice, and we talked about building homes, and he could tell I knew quite a bit about it. In California, we started the mass production of track homes and some of the concepts had not reached Texas yet, which is where he built homes before Guadalajara and that he was very interested in speeding up production. He pointed out that the Adobe Mansions he was building here were nothing like all the stick homes we were building in California.

I had rented a condo in Guadalajara for a few days and stayed and dated Jenifer and her sister. We traveled around the area. The girls knew it very well. We had a good time with the Ruins, the mariachi's day and night, and beer. After a few days, I kissed and hugged them goodbye and jumped on a flight back to Puerto Viarta and Delmar.

We waited a couple more days on the beach, and then Paulo came over and said for us to come over to the shop. They had something for us. We drove over and pulled into the back of the shop. We loaded the kilos up and drove them over to Casa Palomar. We spread them out and opened one up. It was almost sopping wet. This is what happens when you package weed before it is properly dried. I knew these guys were not dealers, so I was not shocked. I think they rushed it too much. Casa

Palomar had a large roof and was directly under the approach path to the airport, and nobody on the airplanes could see the roof except the pilots, and they should be looking at the runway. I was thinking that the hot sun on the roof would dry them out in a couple days. We had the highest house on the hill, so nobody on the ground could see or smell what was on the roof. We turned them over and dried them and repackaged them. The weed was just not sweet because it had gotten damp and not dried properly, but it would get you good and high, and that was the point. I had built a compartment behind the seat in the cab of the truck, and we placed the grass in the compartment and locked it down. We said goodbye to all were friends. I gave Alfonso a small hand half full of sunshine at least a hundred or more hits and said I would return. I told him, "Thank you, and I have your number at the shop. Now maybe I can call ahead and see if they can buy the grass earlier so it can dry properly." We started out driving north to the border nonstop except for gas and snacks. We got close to the border. It was 2:00 a.m. Along the border, we got stopped by the soldiers. They had a roadblock set up. I could hear a generator running, and soldiers came out with automatic weapons and surrounded the truck. One soldier came out with a trouble light, one light bulb on a cord, and tore up my camper. They searched everything. He opened up every cabinet every nook and cranny, and they all were visibly and vocally upset, as I understand curse words in Spanish fairly well and have used them. They could not find anything and told us to drive off. They thought they had made the megalode of drug interception when we pulled up at that early in the morning. This is when only the bad guys are out. Bad judgment on my account. I should have pulled over at a gas stop and slept a few hours. They wanted us gone. We could see another truck pulling up. The soldier gave us our visas and papers back and waved us off. They did not even look in the cab that was where all the stash was. They did not even stick their heads in the cab. It could have smelled. It was a miracle they did not stop us while we were smoking. I had a spray, but there would have been no time to use it. We could not see them until we were right on them. Sometimes I was lucky, and I think my broken Spanish was just enough for him to think that I was a good rich tourist and did not really want to go through an international scene. The peso was really down, and the tourist business was the best for them.

We continued along the border for a couple hundred more miles all day and no Federales. We pulled into John's fathers walled-in estate in almost downtown Tijuana with a large garage. John drove us to Escondido, and we picked up my new Malibu and drove back to Tijuana to get the weed. We dressed up really nice, and John took our wheels of and packed them with the pot. We crossed the border after about ten beers at a Tijuana strip bar and drove right through the customs. They did not want to spoil the fun of a couple of drunk rich kids that came down south for some drinks and fun.

When I was a kid of fifteen, I started coming down here and party. The customs never stopped us at all. When the window opened, the smell of beer and alcohol was predominant. And you just have to look in the customs guys' eyes and act a little messed up, and they just wave you through. We drove over to Chula Vista. I had a house for sale there with a big garage and tools to change tires and remove the weed, and put it back together, then of we went to my ranch in Valley Center. Let the celebration begin. The next day, I drove up to Laguna and dropped off forty pounds to Ro ho. Then I drove over to Anaheim to drop of a few pounds to Butch.

I started thinking about my next trip to Mexico now that I had two good connections, Ricardo and Jenifer. Jenifer went to the American school in Guadalajara. She said all cartels kids go there and she could get me anything I wanted, anytime. Having lots of sunshine had really given me an advantage in Mexico. After they try it, they believed me and were respectful as I was to them. All the people were very confident that I was not a narc. And they were not afraid to introduce me to their friends. I know somehow, I need more friends that go to the American school or who had gone there; it was some kind of cool click. I had found some very wealthy kids. The family was in the oil business, or the entertainment, or the stock markets. They all went nuts for the sunshine. It's the only acid I ever had and known, and I never knew someone who had a bad trip on sunshine. When you were in the business, whenever you hear somebody had a bad trip, I have to ask what acid, and no one ever said sunshine. I have gone out with some of these kids, and I was in my late twenties. I was invited to a wedding party, and all the cool men and I went to the back of their house and fired a machine gun he got for a wedding present. All these kids mostly in their twenties, early or late, and all dressed very fine. All these kids looked up to Americans, but some Americans did not look up to them, and that was a problem sometimes, but not with me. They were very kind to me after knocking their socks off with sunshine they trusted me big time. They all made for very good friends.

After all, the weed was sold. I started to leave to go back to Mexico with more money and my lime green Malibu. I did not need a truck now, just fast wheels. It was a long drive, but I could speed a lot on a few straight roads. There were no police except in the towns that you would ever see. When I pulled into Puerto Vallarta. the first thing I did was drive over to Ricardo's shop, and it was all boarded up. I looked around for a while and was wondering about all the acid I have given him when I left town. I hope it did not get him into trouble. I know he was hooked up pretty good because he had a lot of nice things. I looked over at the El Bandido Bar across the parking lot and was thinking it was about time for a beer. I started walking over there and was thinking Dr. David would know where Ricardo went to.

I walked in and asked the Lady at the door if Dr. David was in. She said he was and asked me to have a seat and she would see if he was available. He came out before I got my beer and had a piece of paper with him. I got up, and we did a little abrazo Mexican thing—I like it. It's just more human than just a handshake. David made a motion with his hand, and a server came over. David ordered a couple shots of tequila and let the evening begin. Before I asked about Ricardo, David gave me this envelope from Ricardo. I opened it up, and Ricardo said that he had moved to Guadalajara and opened up a store there with the address and phone number. It also said for me to please come and see him. It was getting late, and I decided to spend the night in Puerto Vallarta and drive up to Guadalajara in the morning. The roads were not that good, especially at night. Doc invited me to stay at his casa what a spread he had. The house was on a side of a hill with a view of the Pacific and the little Fishing Village, Puerto Vallarta, that was growing big time. The pool was part of the house—indoor and outdoor swimming.

The next day, I called Ricardo in Guadalajara to say hello and tell him I was back in Puerto Vallarta and would be driving up to visit him. He said he was glad to hear from me and he had someone that wanted to meet me. This got me a little excited to see who this could be. The road to Tepic is a winding road up a mountain with a cliff on one side. After you get to the top, the road levels and straightens out as you descend into the valley where Guadalajara is.

I pulled into a large Pemex station when I arrived in town and purchased a street map. Then I found the street that Ricardo's shop was on. It was not hard to find. It was in a nice area, and the front doors and entryway were about twenty feet tall. It was very deluxe with lots of mannequins and shelves full of his clothes that he designed. I left him with two or three hundred little orange barrels. I can only think this might have helped him move up in the Jalisco design world.

We did the normal Mexican greeting with a handshake, and he walked me around the store a little, and we went through a small garden and his office. We sat down and talked about the trip and told me that he always had this store in Guadalajara and was opening up another one by the beach to sell his beach clothes. He said all the sunshine he took back to Guadalajara on the weekend all of his friends in the Bohemian community ate up. He said even friends he had from Mexico City were driving up, and he had just run out of acid.

He asked me if I had brought any sunshine, and I said, "Of course," and reached into my travel bag and brought out a small baggie about the size of a D cell battery. It had 500 hits in it. I tossed it to him, and I asked him if he had a lead on someone that could score lots of weed for me.

He said better than that. He said that he grew up in Guadalajara and went to the American school. He had a girlfriend Gabriella that he told about me, and her father was the main godfather in the Jalisco Cartel. Ricardo was gay, so I know they were just friends, but I know ladies talk more to gay men about crazy things than to straight men.

Ricardo and I had taken acid together on the beach with several other friends, and after that, we became very close. He told me she was hot and nuts, not get-thrown-in-jail-type nuts, but would-like-skinny-dip-at-any-moment-snort-coke nuts and now LSD nuts. She had told her dad about me, and because I had LSD, he wanted to know about it and to meet me. I told Ricardo that I wanted a thousand pounds of weed and I would send my bus for it. He told me to talk to Gabriela about it.

So now I needed to meet this chick, and I did. She had killer good looks and drove a metallic blue new Corvette. Also I asked him where a good place would be to find a condo. He directed me to Apartamentos Los Rosas. It was on a main boulevard that ran into downtown Guadalajara. And walking distance to a Mexican drive-in restaurant like the bean hut in Anaheim, except their specialty was Hamburgases, not tacos or tostadas. I moved into Los Rosas and had a phone turned on and waited for Ricardo to call me. Two years later, I emerged back in the states with some very connected individuals of friends in Mexico and also some wild stories about working for the cartels, Gabriella, and the Mecca of Drugs in Guadalajara.

CHAPTER 5

Pirates Attack

After my first load, I needed a way to import more weed with what means I had available at the time. Then my thoughts turned to the desert, I have spent many nights there. I liked the Yuma Arizona area because it was out in the middle of nowhere and on the border. I wanted to take flying lessons, and Yuma would be a good place for that, and I could find a route to cross over the border from the air.

After my first day, I purchased an air chart of the area. I noticed that most of the mountain ranges ran north and south, and also there was a Navy bombing range east of Yuma, and the Vietnam war was raging. I had been riding motorcycles since I was ten, a long time, and when the Japanese began building dirt bikes, I began buying them. The first ones I broke. Then in 1968, Yamaha built one called a 250 Enduro. I could not break this motorcycle, and it was reliable. I could strap on two twenty-five-pound saddlebags and a fifty-pound backpack. I could carry a hundred pounds of weed across most high desert landscapes, and if chased, I could drop the load quick and haul ass if need be. Most people do not know when you were in the middle of the desert with a little moon, you can see very well the cactus would have shadows after your eyes adjust with no lights. I think it would be impossible to catch me here.

I live within an hour from the desert, and I loved to ride, and I had some friends that loved and did desert cross country racing. I never did that, but I could keep up with the guys that did or beat them occasionally. We raced all weekend. Sometimes we would surprise people camped out in dry riverbeds at night. They would hear us coming and scramble. Also, cold beer on the desert is exceptionally good.

My idea was to drive the weed up to the border and take it across the desert on a motorcycle. Then take it to my house in Yuma and prepare it to transport to Orange County in an airplane or whatever. There was a produce check entering California to help stop the flow of drugs, but I know ways around them, and so did the border patrol, so sometimes they would drive out there and sit and wait for a suspicious vehicle to drive by.

I had two ways to bring five hundred pounds up to the border. One was the bottom of a sixteen-foot outboard boat. On the way north, full of weed at a road construction job by a bridge, the boat fell off the trailer, slid down the embankment, and did not break open. The villagers helped lift pull and drag the boat up the hill and onto the trailer, and we completed the trip. We left the ski boat trailer and motor in the desert after unloading it after that trip. At some point, I was going to write about divine intervention.

Camping with 500 pounds.

The other way to bring weed up to the border is the top of a roll-up camper trailer. Both worked several times. I purchased this camper trailer new, pulled it over to my house, and ripped all the canvas and framework out of the top of the trailer so the bricks could be in the top area, and if you open the door on the lower half and bend over and investigate inside the trailer, you only see the camping things and you must crank the top up to see the weed. We pulled it up to the border. The drivers sometimes would stay at a motel in San Luis Rio, Colorado, and drive out of town a few miles and take a road north a mile and meet me or whoever was riding and load up the weed and go back and vacation a couple nights and then do it again. Sometimes my friends would help, and there would be more than one rider. That made me enough money to buy a ketch—the Kona Mauri a 45' Custom ketch built in Lawndale California for a well-known music composer from Los Angeles.

Kona Mauri Documented Vessel

Cruising

After a long trip

The ketch was beautiful, not so much when I found it. The composer's wife died aboard (RIP) the ketch when they were anchored in Ensenada Bay vacationing. Kona Mauri was the name on the transom. I was told the name was Tahitian. It was left abandoned for about a year. It dragged the anchor and washed up on a beach in the Ensenada Harbor. That's when I purchased it from an insurance company for $25,000. This would be my way to bring tons of pot into the USA.

Loving the weather down south

My plan was to sail out one or two hundred miles out to sea before sailing north up the coast. Then I would plot a course that looked like I was coming from Hawaii, not Mexico. I joined the Kona Kia Yacht club, which was the most exclusive one in San Diego. It had a guard at the gate. It was located next door to the San Diego Coast Guard Station on Shelter Island, which was hide in plain sight with a bright orange and white Yacht club flag on the bow. That's all the San Diego Coast Guard would recognize on the high seas. They do not want to pull us over and search. I would never bring a load into San Diego Bay because there were thousands of miles of coastline. It is easy to find a place to unload and not be noticed. And I did many times. I started bringing the loads to Catalina, and my brothers' friend's dad 25' cabin cruiser, and he would take the weed to Long Beach Harbor, then unload it, and return for more trips. The second time after I did it, I wanted to have the bottom of my ketch painted. So after, I unloaded the weed at Catalina and I sailed it into a boat yard in Long Beach. They hauled it out of the water and put it up on blocks. I had room to park a truck on each side. They never went inside the boat.

Painting boat hull

The boat was now about twenty feet in the air. You need a long ladder to get in. The boat yard only worked on the bottom and never had a reason to go inside the boat. I worked and unloaded all my clothes, guns, food, beer, and things I took for the trip. By now, it was five o'clock, and every one of the workers was all leaving. In a little while, we were all alone in the large boat yard. I started thinking, *Why don't I just sail in here after I return from Mexico. Then have my boat hauled, then pull my trucks in after five o'clock, and unload my weed after the yard closes. I could skip the Catalina part and save a few days on the trip and have the yard do some work on the bottom of my boat.* Never have I got out of a boat yard for less than five thousand. I could eat off the bottom of the boat. Now it's so clean, and being clean means a lot for my overall speed. My ketch was built for pleasure, not for speed. I had the lock combination to get in the boat yard gate anytime. So the last time we did it with the cabin cruiser, it broke down on the way in to unload, and a police helicopter flew over them and asked if they needed help. They yelled okay and waved them off. Then the chopper flew off, and they fixed a loose wire or something and made it into the dock and unloaded it safely.

While the Kona Mauri was having her engine rebuilt scraping and painting the hull, I had an autopilot installed along with a Kelvin Hugh's Radar with a forty-mile ring. Then I had them install stainless steel lifelines and stanchions, so I wouldn't fall off at sea in bad weather and in case I did I towed a one-hundred-foot line.

I had to make a trip deep into Mexico by land to buy and arrange to pick up 3,000 pounds of nice smoke. I needed to buy a sixteen-foot skiff and take it to Mexico so I can move the weed out to the ketch. On the drive down to Mexico, I was going about eighty, and the skiff blew off the truck and landed on its bow. First thing I did when I arrived in Guadalajara was call Daniel, my girlfriend's brother. He was an engineer and a contractor. He arrived at my girlfriend's house and picked up the boat and put it in a truck, and in a couple hours, it was repaired and returned.

Now I needed to go out to the ranchos and purchase more weed. Then I would need to send the weed to my house in Puerto Vallarta Casa Palomar to stockpile it. I would take the skiff down there and prepare for my ketch to come down to pick up the load. On my yacht, I have a Sabot Lifeboat and a Zodiac rubber lifeboat, but they would not haul many pounds. This skiff would carry several hundred pounds at a time. We only wanted to be close to shore for a few minutes even at night. I continued to have the weed all ready to pick up with some fresh food and cold beer. When I had everything set up in Mexico, I parked my truck in Guadalajara and caught the next plane north to San Diego. After I got a good night sleep, I drove over to the yacht club with all my traveling things to leave for the trip. I had fueled the ketch before I went to Mexico, so it would be ready to go when I returned. I had turned two large water tanks into fuel tanks so I could travel all the way to Puerto Viarta and back without refueling. The four-cylinder Ford Osco diesel engine sips fuel. The boat is a motor sailor.

After I was all loaded up with beer and food, I cruised out of San Diego Bay and headed southeast. I wanted to get away from the coast 1970 as there were still a lot of pirates in the waters off the coast of Mexico. I always thought they were the fishermen. Every year back to 1950 that I can remember, there were several incidents where people sailed off to Mexico and never returned. The reason I think was that the fishermen were the pirates. I came in contact with a fishing boat way out to sea. They were slow but can easily overtake a sailboat. He started to pull up beside me. I was about a hundred miles offshore.

South bound cleaning gear

They started yelling, "Do you have food and water?" I went down into the cabin and got out my AR-15. I was an armorer in the Army and could work on most guns. There is a part in most automatic weapons, and it is called a trigger sear. It is what catches the hammer when it comes back after being fired and stops the gun from firing again. I grinded the sear down so the rifle would fire automatic until I released the trigger. The fisherman's boat was pulling closer and closer, and they were getting louder, yelling water or food. They were about thirty feet off now, and I fired a burst about ten shots rapidly toward the bow of their boat. It made a quick turn to the port, and the men shut up, and a couple ran up to the bow of the boat to see if they could see any damage. The men were yelling again, so I put down an area of fire toward the front of their old wooden vessel with the rest of my clip. I did not see any wood chips flying. It seemed to get them moving a little faster, and they started trying to hide on the deck from my fire. I could sink their boat if I wanted too, and I had two full cans of bullets.

I have had a few chances to shoot someone, but the thing is that I would never want to hurt anyone. The Ten Commandments were a good thing to follow through life, but I would not go down in Mexico without a huge fight. The fisherman figured it out and left the scene as fast as they could. I noted the name on the boat but never did anything about it. I wasn't worried about them. I think if they ever saw my ketch again, they would turn away. After a little work and modifications, I had rigged my ketch so I could sail it all by myself. I had autopilot and Kelvin Hugh's Radar with a forty-mile ring, as well as an old wind-up alarm clock. I could run all twenty-four hours a day and night. At night when ships could not see me, I could set the alarm clock for two hours and sleep. Then when the alarm went off, I woke up look at the radar screen if it showed me if there was anything within forty miles of me, and if clear, I went back to sleep. Sometimes at night when sailing, looking on the radar screen, I could watch the large ocean liners changing course like twenty miles out of their way to go way around me. They could see me well because I had my radar on day and night and it acted like a transponder and lit up their radar screen, so they could see something. Most people don't know as when these ships get too close to smaller vessels at speed. Their wake is like a title wave and can swamp small vessels. Most of the shipping lanes noted on sea charts were usually easy to avoid with a little navigating skill no GPS.

After the encounter with the fishermen, I changed my course more to the east to run a little closer to shore. As I got closer to Puerto Vallarta, the winds changed and started coming from the south. It started to get warmer and smelled a little different. I started playing with the automatic direction finder and wanted to come into the Puerto Vallarta area from a direct line from the west fifty miles out to avoid any Mexican Navy vessels that could be cruising the coast as I had no visa, but I had a documented vessel, and with the American flag, this vessel cannot be boarded by any nation. Who knows how that could be enforced out at sea?

After locating myself with two radio beacons and decided I was about twenty-five miles out, I started calling my crew onshore with the weed with a high-frequency radio. They came back on the first call loud and clear and sounded as if they were real glad to hear from me. I can imagine they have been sitting out in the jungle with two trucks and three thousand pounds of pot for a few days. I planned to make shore around dusk so we could load after dark. As I sailed closer to the shore, the wind was dying down, and it looked like the surf was about two feet perfect for this operation.

I was using the depth sounder, checking the bottom looking for about twenty-five feet water depth, and I found it about one hundred feet offshore, and I could see a flashlight coming from the beach, and that's my crew. They rowed out to meet me and got ready to load. I lowered my Zodiac with its small motor into the water so we could load the Zodiac and the skiff with weed and pull the skiff out to the ketch with the Zodiac and its outboard motor.

This is hard work

We were moving several hundred pounds of weed at a time. But it still took several hours to load it and stash it inside my ketch. We were a hundred miles from nowhere. There were no lights anywhere we could see. All the stars were very bright. The crew had all the fresh food and beer for my return trip.

After we loaded, we drank and ate and celebrated a little, and then I started everything up and started sailing back to California. I started to get comfortable for a long ride home with a slight hangover. It's good. I like to read and have many paperbacks and a nice overseas radio for music, news, and sometimes old weather observations.

I was starting by sailing north by northwest for a few days and then north for many days. All smooth sailing, I just saw a few large ocean freighters and one fairly large Schooner that was running south and fast with the winds. I had made a tentative reservation at the Long Beach boat yard to clean and paint my boats bottom with antifouling paint.

After I was north of San Diego about a day out of Long Beach, I called the shipyard on the ship to shore radio and told them approximately what time I would arrive the next day. It' easy to figure out. It takes ten hours to sail from San Diego to Catalina Island. I was going to drop my anchor at the Catalina Isthmus, twenty-six miles of the coast of California, and spend the night. Then I was going to sail into Long Beach Harbor the next afternoon, which was about five- or six-hour trip.

I called my ground crew after I came ashore at the Isthmus to meet me at the house, and they knew what that meant—to meet me at the boat yard after it closes at five. Also, they should drive around some to make sure they were not followed.

The sailboat worked for a couple years, but my head was in the sky. I had plenty of money to buy an airplane. Now I needed to learn how to fly. The Yuma Airport was a great place. It was busy with Navy aircraft traffic mostly from Miramar

Naval Air Station just over the mountains on the west side. A few minutes travel time in an F-4, I found a flight office at the airport and a flight instructor. He had a piper 140, the most basic of airplanes. It was a cool place to learn—all desert, nothing to run into. I wanted to learn to fly fast. I had weed waiting for me. So I did not work. I went to the airport almost every day to fly. The instructor was good, and after eight hours, he told me I was ready to solo. We landed at this triangle runway near the Yuma Airport. It was a safety landing strip for the Navy. There was nothing around here except soft sand, what a place for a crash? After we landed a couple times, he climbed out of the airplane and said, "It's time for you to solo." I was a little scared but tried not to show it, wondering how we would get back to the airport if I crash. The flight went well. I made a couple more takeoffs and landings. Then he motioned for me to pick him up, and we flew back to the Yuma Airport. I had friends and relatives that had airplanes, so they all let me fly some on trips that helped a lot.

When you get a solo license, it is part of a medical exam form. So all I had to do was have my instructor sign me off, and he did. Now I have a solo license, but I could not carry passengers. No one would rent me an airplane without more training, and I would have to jump through a bunch of hoops. However I could buy one and not have to take a test or more training. I would teach myself and get a license later. I did not need a license for the type of flying I wanted to do anyway. I moved over to the coast and started flying at Marten Aviation at the Santa Ana Airport. I met the best instructor they had. His name was Dean Englhart, and he flew helicopters also and did stunt work for Hollywood movies. My father told me that if I wanted to be a real pilot, I should learn in a taildragger. So I told Dean I wanted to buy a tailwheel airplane. He said no problem and that I should buy a Cessna 170 for it would carry four passengers. It was the best, all aluminum and tough for off-field landing. That's all he needed to say, and we were looking for a 170.

We started my flying lesson by flying to all the airports in the Los Angeles Basin. I was amazed at how easy it was to travel around Los Angeles—so easy above all that traffic. In most of the area, you just must stay below three thousand feet to stay out the restricted airspace. Also stay above all the little airport traffic areas. They were spaced apart enough—you can just drive around them.

My first airplane.

After about a week, we found a red and white Cessna 170 at the El Monte Airport. They wanted $6,500. I offered them $5,000 and got up. They also got up and said they would take $5,500. I gave them $500 in cash and said, "I will be back tomorrow with the rest of the money." They made all the paperwork a simple bill of sale. The next day, I had another pilot fly to El Monte with Dean and me. We got up there in less than an hour. I counted out the rest of the money to the salesman.

I knew Dean could fly taildraggers. and off we went. I was at the controls. It was scary, but I managed to stay on the runway until I accelerated enough to fly. Then it was just like any other airplane. I had reserved a parking spot on the ramp at the Santa Ana Airport to keep my 170.

After we landed, we parked it on my spot at the Santa Ana Airport for the first time, and I took a picture. I know it was 1969 because my new Malibu was in the picture. I told Dean I was going to clean it up and work around it for a while. He told me, "Whatever you do, do not fly this airplane without me."

I told him, "Don't worry about it. I won't fly it." I do not like to lie, but this was different—my new airplane. I found myself standing on my toes, looking out over the parking lot to see if Dean was gone. After I saw him drive away, I called for the fuel truck and top off my new-to-me airplane. Airplanes were not like cars. They appreciate instead of depreciate. This Cessna is a 1954 model one of the last airplanes built before tricycle landing gear was generally used. It is a little faster than the newer models. The airplane was taken good care of, and all I could do was polishing it some.

After I was sure he was gone, I called one of my friends to come over for airplane ride. He lived in Laguna and took a little while to arrive. When he arrived, I let him in the gate at the parking lot, and we started the airplane up. I called for taxi clearance and was told to taxi to the widest runway. It was two or three hundred feet wide, and I used all of it to takeoff. At this time, I had about sixteen hours total flight time with an instructor. The takeoff scared both of us. John said, "WTF, I thought you knew how to fly."

I said, "I do, but the takeoffs and landings need help."

We flew out toward Catalina Island. We could see it easily it was a perfect California day, a little smoke in the air but real good views on the coast. I knew the island fairly well as sometimes I would leave my ketch anchored there for a week or two and fly back and forth with a charter flight out of Santa Ana or seaplane out of long beach. One time, the Harbor master at Avalon called me and said it looked like my yacht was sinking. I drove to Long Beach and caught the next seaplane to Avalon. When I arrived, I could see that my ketch was very low in the water. I flagged down a water taxi. He took me out to my boat. I jumped on the ketch and looked into the cabin. The floor was covered with water up to the floor boards. I started up the Onan Generator to charge the batteries, then went down into the cabin and started closing all valves, and turned on the bilge pumps. The water in the engine room was about six inches below the dipstick tube. If seawater gets into the engine, it will ruin it. I checked the oil, and there was no water in it. Thankfully I got there in time. I started the diesel engine. It purred like a little kitten. I checked the oil again, and there was no brown foam. I was very glad that I arrived in time to close all the through hull fittings until I found the one that failed. After sailing back to San Diego, I had all the valves below deck replaced with new fittings.

After flying around the island a couple times, I lined up on the runway at Catalina, and as I got closer to the runway, the wind was tossing me around, and the runway looked short, and at the end of the runway was a cliff—bad news. If you were too fast, you could go over the edge and crash, so as I got closer, I could tell this was not going to work, so I decided to go around and fly back to Santa Ana and land on the big runway. My landing at Santa Ana was funny if you were not in the cockpit. I landed several times and used the entire runway on that landing one side to the other. I think they were laughing in the tower. After a while, I got better but still needed more practice. I was on my way to my airplane as I passed the chief instructor at Marten Aviation. He said to me, "I watched you

land and wanted to know if you wanted some more instruc-
tion." At that time, I was thinking they wanted to know if I had
a pilot's license. I was practicing landings at the Huntington
Beach Airport, a small grass strip. I was better at landing and
takeoffs now, so I moved my airplane over to the Huntington
Beach Airport.

I was getting a whole lot better flying and landing, and a
taildragger would teach you all about the wind. You just have to
be able to live through it. I started landing on roads and fields,
even dry lakes and a bridge. I started thinking I could fly now
and could stop using the Kona Mauri, my sailboat, and do trips
now in one day, not one month. I was most comfortable near a
beach, and I knew a few in the Baja that I could land on. Now
I must see how far my Mexicans could bring weed up north
for me. I was letting my brothers from Laguna know that I was
going to start airplane service to Baja. I think after selling tons
of my weed off my boat. Smity or somebody decided to buy
their own sailboat, but they had bigger plans with it that didn't
work out that well. They were gone for a long time on their first
trip. It lasted much longer than they planned. They did not
leave enough money for their families in Laguna, so I went up
there every week or so to give Rosy a kilo of pot. Rosy told me
they had no money and were selling the pot at the Taco Bell to
eat. I told her I would give her more if she wanted. She said she
didn't want to fool around with all that. They were fine with
a kilo at a time. Having those brothers gone cut down on my
sales, but the commodity was always wanted somewhere. The
brothers I have known since school in Anaheim, and I know
they were not snitches, and when I fronted them tons, they
would not ever testify against me, and I would get paid.

My Mexican allies do not want to leave their comfort
zones, so I would organize a ground trip to pick up five hundred pounds and take it to the border so I could pick it up and

bring it back to Ocotillo Wells dry lake. The easiest was to use my bus, which was nothing like a VW camper. This bus had an all-steel body; you could put a couple VW campers inside it. It was built by Chrysler on a big Dodge truck frame. I remodeled the inside and made a compartment that would hold five hundred kilos. It worked several times Kilo John used it once.

I sent the bus down to Guadalajara to bring the kilos up to San Luis Rio, Colorado, and I had found a good dirt road I could land on near there. I would take several five-gallon gas cans full of fuel to pour in my tanks when I landed. I would need the fuel to get home on. The inside of an airplane full of gas smelled like a bomb. It could be with a spark. The good part was that as soon as you were cruising, the smell with the fumes moved to the back of the airplane so the smoking lamp is on. All this worked good for a while, but I was getting tired of flying all night with a single-engine airplane. If the engine quits, it's bad news. If the engine in a twin-engine airplane fails, you can keep flying and get home.

I needed to buy a fast twin-engine airplane and be able to carry more weight and go farther into Mexico. I always worried about my people being caught driving the weed up to the border, and with fast twin with long legs, they could all stay home and sell pot. I have been very lucky as I have driven weed up to the border, and it was very scary. I have never been caught nor has anyone that worked for me. I have been in a Mexican jail for other things, but I would never go back. I flew Jack and Smitty down to Hermosillo prison for someone they knew that got caught for something. There were a lot of stories about Mexican prisons none were good. I was very lucky.

CHAPTER 6

Oaxaca Express

I kept pushing my income tax trial back for about a year. I was trying to increase my cash flow problems. I had a large amount of cash in my barn. It was lost during a raid on my ranch. The Internal Revenue Service had my bank accounts on hold. I needed to raise fifty thousand to pay my attorney to handle my income tax evasion trial. The reason it was so much was that they brought into the team a former Federal assistant attorney that knew the Federal ropes and judges and such. He made a deal for me no more than two years and only six months for good behavior. So I had to be good. Also we had to do a jury trial I guess for show. It lasted a month. George told me because drugs were mentioned at my trial, six thousand pounds of marijuana, that they would test me sometime while I was inside, that if I would smoke some grass and get tested, I would be in jail for the full two years. George made a point not to smoke pot till after I was tested.

The FBI IRS border patrol raided my ranch the night while I was in jail. The Raiders were intent on finding something. They found a lot of cash under a ton of bailed hay in the loft in one of my barns. There was a lot more cash there than what was reported. My attorney friend told me when they captured me at the Fullerton California Airport after I landed. I wasn't being chased, and it was several days since I had been down south. So it had to have been a wiretap. I called Chuck, one of my partners, the night before I landed in Fullerton. I told him I was going to the Fullerton Airport and my approximant time of arrival the next day. It had to have been that call that alerted the heat.

After the trial was finally over like it lasted a month, I was in the local Federal Correctional facility, waiting to be transferred to a Federal prison. I was smoking some Afghanistan hash, the black and soft in my room with the door halfway open. I had fashioned A pipe out of a TV cable connector and some cigarette foil. In the middle of the night, I climbed up and took the cable TV connector of the back of the community TV in the common area. The TV was not working for a couple of days. Then some TV repairman came and just replaced the connector, and nobody ever looked for the part or said anything about the missing connector. TV was on now. This was a joke; they were so lame.

My wife would bring small amounts of Primo hash in her cheek. It was fresh and soft and strong. It only took a couple hits to launch. She could visit me every night while I was waiting to be transferred. She would pass it to me when we kissed or held hands. So later I was upstairs in my room with the door open a little, and a guard just happened to pass by on his rounds and smelled the hash smoke. He stuck in his head in the door and could see me smoking the hash. He rushed in and grabbed me, and we went to the floor, me swallowing the hash as he was trying to stop me. He had about a hundred pounds on me. We started to tussle a little, and there was no way I was going to let him get the hash. Somehow I swallowed the hash and lost the pipe pieces somewhere.

We ended up on the floor, and the only thing he had was a small piece of stained tinfoil. He wasn't mad, and neither was I. It wasn't like I was fighting him. He just said he was going to write a report and file it in the morning and maybe get a tetanus shot. He left the room, and I do not think anybody else even knew it happened. I might have bit him. It all happened in just a couple of minutes.

This was a big deal because if he filed the report, I would not get out in six months. So I went to talk to the local jailhouse lawyer in the next cell. He told me that if I could get transferred to my prison, where I would be doing my time in the morning, any reports about me that happened the night before the transfer would not travel with me to the new Federal prison. Saved again! I had another call to my attorney Joe. He said he would call the judge and have me transferred to Terminal Island Federal Penitentiary in the morning. This was late at night now, but he called the judge and got it done. This attorney is one of my favorites. He is a retired assistant Federal attorney that is liked by all the attorneys and is good friends with all the judges, and he is very wealthy.

Somehow later they transferred the guard that tussled with me up to Terminal Island with me. The first time I saw him, I was walking around the yard with a joint in my pocket, looking for a place or a girl to smoke it with. We made eye contact, his expression didn't change, and I was ready to eat the joint and go down to the ground again; he wasn't. Terminal Island is a country club prison—tennis, softball, golf, and mostly important women. You have to be careful though for one of the Manson girls was here. I didn't think the Nazi sign scar on her forehead was very attractive.

While I was out on bail waiting for this tax trial to start, I partied for about six months between Hawaii Southern California and Mexico, and I needed to do some flying. Medicine without borders needed to start a scam. I declared marijuana as medicine from Mexico to Texas. I was too hot to do anything in California and Arizona. Sometimes the cops followed me whenever I got near an airport, and they were not even shy about it. I have not done the Texas route for a while. The weed flavor of the day from Mexico was called Baseball Bats. This was like two or three feet long pot stalks covered with big colas as big as a fist, almost as big as the hash buds that made Primo hash, which came in sometimes from Afghanistan. These Baseball Bats would pack easily into my trash compactor bags.

This brand of weed is found in Oaxaca, Mexico, the home of Mescal, the worm in the bottle high test drink. They have here in Oaxaca what's called mezcalitos. They were lying by the side of the streets early in the mornings after drinking Mescal all night. Some say it is a little psychedelic. I say it's a killer hangover.

I needed to raise some money to put down on the load and pay for airplane gas and others. I needed at least 500 kilos; one or two thousand would be better. I have good credit. Probably I would need at least 50 percent to swing the load. It took about three months to put the deal together. Find the cash to put with my cash travel back and forth from Los Angeles to Oaxaca. Renting a house in Oaxaca. sometimes I would go out in the fields to meet the farmers and give them some money to start acquiring the weed and storing it until we were ready. Everything was moving along. I had the airplane picked out to fly the load. The crew in Texas was ready to go, but the packaging was taking way too long and my trial was coming up.

I decided I should go to Oaxaca and try and speed things up. This scam had to be complete before my trial started, or my attorney would be a little unhappy, and so would I especially if I had to go to prison immediately after the trial was over. I would lose the load if I couldn't pick it up.

On my way to Oaxaca on the drive to LAX Airport, I stopped by a Sears Roebuck store and purchased another trash compactor to go with the one I previously sent down with my crew to Oaxaca. The compactors made a perfect twenty-five-pound square container and perfect to pack fast. I checked the compactor at the airport as baggage. It is in its original box. If anyone would say anything, I would say it was for my house down in Mexico. If they said, "Do you need a hundred bags?"

I would say, "I do not come stateside often." No one ever said anything about the compactor or the boxes of bags, even the Aduana. The Mexican customs officer even carried it out for me and put it in the trunk of my rental car. He would remember the tip I gave him for a very long time. He was so happy when he waved goodbye at 3:00 a.m.

The city Oaxaca is the capital of the state of Oaxaca. It is beautiful mild temperatures in mountains and Mayan ruins and pyramids. I was driving around Oaxaca, looking for our house with the trash compactor sticking out of the trunk of my car. I don't think that it stuck out at all at 3:00 a.m. It was very dark here at night, not lit up like the states. I passed a few mezcalitos on the side of the road and thought I might have hit a curb.

When I arrived at the house, everyone was asleep around 4:00 a.m. But I have been sleeping for several hours. I really could sleep good on an airplane like deep sleep. My trial was coming up. I needed to get these guys going. It didn't take long to find out what caused the slowdown, when Squeaky John pulled out a bag with about a quarter pound of coke in it and started passing it around. There must have been ten cases of beer stacked up and tequila bottles and empty bottles everywhere. We sat down and drank and smoked for a while. Then Squeaky John told me one night when they were bringing some weed to the house, they had to run a road block, the soldiers fired just one shot, and it hit JB, which killed him. JB and I went to school together in Anaheim. He was I think the nicest brother. I never asked John any details because I have enough things to worry about. Squeaky John said JB wasn't working the scam. He just came down for the excitement or just wanted to see how it was done.

It was a real zoo. We had me, squeaky John, Gabby, Felipe, and Pulga. These guys were so cool. All they want was money and fun, and they had the money. I let them use my Eldorado convertible one time on one of their visits to the West Coast. It started raining. They tried to put the top down going sixty-five miles per hour. It didn't take long! It never did work right after that. I have more cars, no big deal. They probably risk their lives in the jungles, buying weed for me, so I could pay for the mellow yellow Eldo. They said I should have told them about the top. They were right. I guess I was not used to people who do not know how to operate a drop-top.

The house sat on top of a hill on a box canyon with nice-size houses not too close together, covering the Canyon Walls on both sides. It has one road that leads into the canyon. It can be seen from this house, which is perfect if we have to escape. That road leads into several other streets that loop around the canyon on three levels. These roads had street lights that were widely spaced around the streets. They had these big round light bulbs that look like Thomas Edison built them. We started packing all the weed into the bags, compacting them to around twenty-five pounds. Then I overamped the electrical system the first time I pushed the start button on the new compactor when the other one was compacting. The increased electrical load overamped the electrical system, and the whole canyon went dark—street lights and everything else, most importantly our house and the compactors. The main circuit breaker had to be reset to turn the electric back on. I think it was probably at the bottom of the hill. We waited for about twenty minutes, and the power would come back on.

We decided that we had to be very careful with the compactors not running them at the same time. Beer, tequila, weed, and other things made it very hard to not trip the main circuit breaker. It happened a couple more times. Then I told the guys we need to knock off for a while. I was worried about arousing the authorities. I worked the next day with the guys. I noticed working around the house there was a lot more weed there than just a thousand pounds. I asked Gabby about it, and he said he had more because he wanted to make sure he had enough. It turned out he was accumulating four thousand pounds or more. I found out later when they wanted me to fly the extra weed. The next night, I jumped a flight back to Los Angeles.

My income tax trial was very close now. I had to wait for the amigos to finish packing the weed. Then they had to drive the weed across Mexico to Yucatan where we had a long grass strip. They also needed to talk to the local farmers around the area to see if there was any military action around the runway. It belongs to the Mexican Army. They only use it for training sometimes. The local farmers knew when they would be training there and when they wouldn't be training there. We always paid them for their information. They were very poor. The Army never gave them anything.

I was down to the wire, and the trial would start in one week. I was talking to my attorneys almost every day. I could not get a hold of Gabby. I think he was traveling in between Oaxaca Yucatán. And I hope he was all right. I have been trying to have my attorneys put the trial off for thirty days. They got back to me quickly and said we already had a year before the trial and some of the feds were wondering why I was still out and running around. And that I would go immediately to prison after the trial.

I have been wondering why my legal team had not been asking me for the $25,000 balance. I owed them for this trial. But we have done a lot of business before, and being friends, they just didn't say anything. I needed a little more time to pay the money, and if I didn't get the time to fly the load, I probably wouldn't be able to pay the balance at all. Finally Gabby arrived in Merida Yucatán, his home, which was within two hundred miles from the grass strip. I called him and told him it would be a couple days for me to set up and be there. I called my attorney and explained to him the night before the trial that I did not have the $25,000 and if I did not get any more time to pick the load up, I would never be able to pay him. He told me to be hopeful and do the best I could.

I checked into a nice downtown five-star hotel with my girlfriend, a real cover girl, the night before the trial started. We were walking through the hotel lobby on the way to a nice downtown restaurant, and I could see Connie getting off an elevator, and I confronted her. She said the reason she was here was to be testifying against me. My attorneys had told me about her. She would testify that she helped me bring six tons of weed into the states on my ketch. Her husband was one of my very best friends. This guy could do anything he wanted to do or fix anything. He was the best carpenter I had in my construction company.

I think sometimes I made flying across the border look easy. But it was not. Dan was one of my first protégés that went on his own and got killed. There were more! Dan, with eight hundred pounds of pot and no fuel, crashed in the desert at night. It took more than just a pilot. It took a good crew to make sure you have what you need like fuel and would die for you, I think but would not bet on the last part, but I never I had to test it. Back at the hotel, I asked Connie to join us for dinner.

Once we were seated and our drinks were ordered, I asked her how she was after Dan died, and I said I was very sorry he was the best. She said she was connected to the crash that led to Dan's death as he was on the way to their ranch in Arizona. They had been running scams out of there for a while, too long

I think. The feds had my number, somehow connected us, and told her if she would testify against me, they would let her off.

We were always good friends for many years, and I was not mad about her testimony. It was all hearsay, no evidence, anyway, but the drug information gave the jury a lot to think about. And this was not the mafia. We do not hurt people. But anyway we had a nice dinner, and we talked about old times and how we used the money we made with the ketch (a ketch is a large two masted sail boat), bringing in tons of smoke from Puerto Viarta, Mexico, to Catalina Island. We sold the tons of weed to buy ranches and airplanes. Dan purchased a ranch in Arizona. I purchased a ranch in California. We went different ways but were very good friends. I felt bad about Dan getting killed in the crash. I was glad Connie would not have to go to jail over this after losing her husband. I wanted to know how he could possibly run out of gas. He was a better of a pilot than this. And somebody down south did not have enough good clean fuel, unless he got shot down, and the feds covered it up. The feds said fuel starvation caused the crash.

I met my attorney in the courthouse before my trial started. He asked me if there was any movement toward the twenty-five thousand I still owed him. I said no, and I explained to him again that if I did not go pick up my load, I would lose all the money I had invested, which was almost fifty thousand. He said he would work with me. We had done a lot of business, and I always paid them. We walked into the courtroom together, and his assistant had our table set up with all the files.

After the trail got started and everyone was introduced and situated, my lawyer said he had to use the restroom. The judge excused him. Everybody just sat there for a while—the judge, the jury, the prosecutors, and the courtroom recorder. The courtroom was fairly full, which surprised me a little. I guess they did not do income tax evasion trials often. We waited for about twenty or twenty-five minutes. I could see the judge was starting to look a little annoyed. Then the assistant US attorney, Mr. Hoover, who lived down the street from me, asked me if I would go and look see what was holding my lawyer up and get him up here.

I got up and walked down stairs where the restrooms where at and went into the first men's room door. A guy was just standing there as if he was waiting for me. He said, "Are you looking for your attorney?"

And I said, "Yes, I am." As I was looking around, not seeing anyone in the room and stalls. I started believing him. He replied that my attorney had heart attack and collapsed in a stall and was taken by ambulance to the hospital. I turned around, and he followed me out of the bathroom. When I made it back upstairs to the courtroom, I walked in, and all eyes were on me you could hear a pin drop.

The judge motioned me forward, and I walked right up to the bench, with the judge close in front of me. I could smell the aftershave and said quietly that my attorney had a heart attack and went to the hospital. The judge sat back in his chair to speak to the court. He thought for a moment and stated that due to my attorney being ill, we would set the trial back thirty days, until we would find out the condition of the defendant's attorney. Then he asked the court reporter for a new trial date. She looked through her book and came up with a date. She gave it to us and asked if it would work for all of us. The prosecutors and my legal team looked at their calendar dinked around for a moment. Then they agreed to the date. It was around thirty days. So we all agreed, and by now, my heart was pounding as I was free for a month. Plane B was just to not show up for my trial one morning and go directly to Mexico. Now I didn't have to go outlaw again. I was pretty sure this whole trial thing was just a show. The legal system would do almost anything to get paid as long as it was all legal. I was pretty sure if I sold hard narcotics, none of this would be going on, and if these guys thought I was selling hard narcotics, they would lock me up. None of them smoked weed, but a couple of them said their wives did for sleep or pain. I gave them a real nice kilo, and it blew their minds.

I walked over to the hotel and checked myself and the other Connie out. We called her Consuela. I dropped her off at her mother's house and then drove out to my ranch. I collected the area charts that I would need, my flight bag, and the things I might need for the trip—about a week supply of clean clothes, shave kit, etc. I never take a life preserver. They were all on my boat.

I cross six hundred miles of sea each way. I always had two engines—what could go wrong? Always at the point of no return, the engines always seemed to be running a little rough. The airplane was only twenty years old. Also I brought a pocket full of joints and stashed an ounce of good bud with some rolling papers all to go to Texas and work. I had pretty much everything ready to go as I had been planning this flight for some time now and had done this flight before, just different landing airports in Texas. I never used the same airport again. There were thousands of airports.

I stopped on the way to my airport and called by pay phone the Texans and said I was on the way. They were a little upset it had been taking so long. I told them I was tied up in the courts, but I was on the way now. I asked them if they were ready. They said, "Bring it on."

The load was waiting for me when I called Gabby the next morning and told him when I would arrive at the grass runway late the next afternoon. They were beyond happy. They have been waiting too long with all that grass and gas. It all smelled big time.

The next late morning, I took off from Texas to Yucatan When I arrived off the coast of Yucatan looking for this runway, I started triangulating my position by using two long-range radio beacons; this was not easy. I just needed to find the general vicinity. It was very hard to find the first time, but not this time. I knew it like the back of my hand. This strip was way out in the middle of the jungle. It's all flat and green, and you could see for hundreds of miles. It looked like a hundred-mile golf course, green from up high. I wonder what the space men thought when they came out of the space and saw all this. In the states, there are usually hills or mountains that you can look at that tell you where you are. I triangulated my position again by using long-range radio waves and got closer to the runway. Then I used my eyes, instinct, and dead reckoning to find the strip. The roads were all grown over, and they were very hard to find from the air; even a small town some time could not be seen.

I radioed my amigos, and they were loud and clear and close. I found the runway and circled and looked for soldiers and trucks but could not see anything, so I landed and parked in the middle of the landing field. I started getting ready for another takeoff and checked the airplane over. The oil was fine. It all looked ready to go. I was standing around the middle of the grass runway. All of a sudden, two black flatbed trucks came flying out of the jungle with a lot of people in the back of both trucks.

My first thought was soldiers. There was no way I could start engines and fly out of there and get away. The trucks were very fast. My other escape would be on foot. But when they got a little closer, I could see them better. They had baseball hats on, not helmets. They were cheering and waving their arms. They were so happy to see me. They had been waiting with a truck full of weed and another truck full of barrels of gas for a while when I was in courtroom. The first guy I talked to was Squeaky John. We shook hands and hugged. They call it abrazo here. He was really funny, pasty skin, blond, and blue. He speaks the best Spanish of the group. He never could roll his Rs while he spoke Spanish. He picked up the name when he was living in Hawaii. Finely after putting everyone to work, it seemed that they were in no hurry.

This made me a little more comfortable that they were not worried about the Army making a raid. They acted like they owned the place—Gabby Felipe and Pulga (which means flea in Spanish). I have been sitting in a chair for several hours and needed a break. And yes, Pulga was very small and very cool like all the other guys in this group—very Cool. They walked up and abrazo shake hands. It had been a few weeks since I have seen him in Oaxaca. He said he was glad to see me, and he said he had 2,000 pounds for me, which was fine. Then he said he had more, but he had to drive back to Oaxaca and bring it back to Yucatan and it would take about a week to get it all together.

So I was thinking all along what took so long and delayed me. It was because they were building another load for someone else, on my dime. Gabby said that I would only get 25 percent of the second or third load because there were more people involved now, and I was thinking Bobby. I told him, "I want half and call me if you can do that." I think they had another way to get it to the states, and at the last minute, that route was shut down for who knows how many reasons. He did not sound too happy about my decision, but so what. We had a couple beers and talked about a few things we had done together. The crew finished the fueling and loading the airplane.

I looked at the plane, and it was sitting so low to the ground. The struts were almost totally collapsed, so I knew it was very heavy and a little over gross. Squeaky John wanted to ride back with me to California. He was a little eccentric. His father was a professor at an Ivy League College. He is a real good fun loving kid. Of course he had on this all white linen suit. He said he had this suit especially made for this trip. It looked really neat but a little wrinkled and dirty, but we were in the middle of a jungle. I told him, "After we land, if you see me start running, you run the opposite direction!" John laughed, but I could see he was thinking about it.

Full fuel, full everything else. It was a ninety-five-degree day, but at least I was at sea level. I knew that I needed a very long runway to get this mess in the air, so I taxied all the way back to the end of the runway, facing into the light wind. I was sure that I was overweight, but I thought it would climb if I could get the landing gear up fast enough after takeoff. Also I knew if I wanted to abort the takeoff, I probably would not be able to stop the aircraft before I ran off the runway at one hundred ten knots into the jungle, so this thing must lift off or die. So I needed to use all the runway and gain the most speed I can get before I rotate. Once we got up into cooler air and burn off some fuel, we could get this old bird rolling again. The takeoff took forever. This runway was one mile long. I locked the brakes up and ran the engines up to full power and released the brakes. The airplane barely started to roll real slow. I had ten knots, twenty knots, thirty knots, and finally forty. The tires were starting to float a little on the wet grass now, and we were accelerating a little faster now. I fought the control to keep going straight down the runway. We were bouncing up and down left and right. The struts were pounding and bottoming out. I could see the end of the runway was coming up. It was now or never. I had to hoarse the plane into the air. I was going to ask John to help me pull back on the yoke, but his eyes were closed, his jaw was clenched, and he had white knuckles on the copilot's seat. He wasn't going to be much help. I found a little more up trim on my trim wheel. I used it. I had about one hundred ten knots on the speedo. I gritted my teeth and pulled back as hard as I could, and we leaped of the ground. I brought the gear up as fast as I could, and I heard the gear motor was operating, and we started to sink.

I pushed the nose over just a little to gain some speed. The wheels were up now. We could start to pick up some speed now. It worked. We stopped the sinking because we were in ground effect. I could feel the plane accelerating. We were in the tops of the palm trees now. The stall warning horn was beeping. As soon as I felt the speed coming on, I quickly pulled back a little on the yoke with the extra speed. It jumped into the sky. Again the horn went silent. I was going to have to clean the windshield. That's how I knew we were in trouble when the palm leaves and the greens of hammock of the jungle started hitting the windshield from the prop wash. There's going to be some green stains to clean and maybe some paint work to do on the fuselage. After that takeoff, it was amazing. I was thinking maybe Gabby might have overloaded me a lot. We were finally on the way to Texas. We started a very slow climb to 10,000 feet and level off. We were flying high to get the good fuel mileage. John had a pocket full of joints. We had a cassette player. We were rocking out to the Stones and Johns tunes and making a suitcase full of money.

It was beautiful up there. There were a few thunder storms, but we were driving around them and it was getting dark. We could see the lightning in the clouds. This was good the border patrol. "Do not fly in this weather." This was before all airplanes had radar. After about three hours, I turned on one of my navigation radios and tuned in the Galveston radio beacon, and it gave me my distance from that station and an arrow in the instrument that pointed to Galveston, Texas. Now I could see where the winds have placed me on the course and adjusted my course for direct Galveston.

When I got to one hundred miles out, I would start a descent and leave the power levers up and gain a lot of airspeed. I would try and make up some of the time we lost in the climb. We were down to one hundred feet now, and salt started to build on the bottom of the windscreen. I think I was squeezing the salt out of the air with the speed. It was growing on the windshield now but would only grow up to about four inches before we landed.

We were cruising through the oil rigs. There were thousands of them, forty or fifty miles off shore. Most people never see them. We were eye level with the rigs. We could even look in some windows sometimes. I don't think they ever reported us. We went so fast. I don't think they had much time to identify the airplane. I was keeping my eyes out for helicopters. They would have their lights on. After about twenty miles, we were starting to see the shoreline lights, and John went to the rear of the plane to change clothes to something dark. I had on all-black clothes. I looked like a server.

We were going to a small town airport. It was selected because the police station was on the other side of town and would take ten minutes to arrive at the airport if called. We could do our thing in five minutes. We would be landing there in the middle of the night, and I have made contact with the ground crew. They were close to the airport, and it was all quiet. I navigated to the airport and circled as I was lining up with the runway that I wanted to use. I did not want to fly over the police station low without lights. I didn't see any strange lights, and my crew was silent, so everything must be fine. I landed without lights and taxied over to a spot behind a hanger.

The crew pulled up right after I shut down, and within a couple minutes, they had my airplane empty and vacuumed out. After all that, John and I flew over to Houston, without incident, and spent the night there. Although there was an incident in the hotel that happened in Houston late that night, it had to do with a stripper and spurs. One off the girls was not a real cowgirl. She forgot where her spurs were at and jumped off the bed and landed on her spurs and started screaming and bleeding. After the hotel security came up, the bleeding slowed down. She assured the security guards that it was an accident and no big deal. Just as the police rolled up with their lights on, one of the security guards went over and talked to the police for about a minute, and they did not waste any time leaving.

She told them what actually happened and showed them her cute little foot. We had about a half pound of grass and a few other things with us. That's why the girls were so happy and a little out of control. They wanted to take us to their apartment and marry us. I must say the ladies in Houston were almost comparable to the ladies off Vegas now. All we had was hundred-dollar bills—the life of an anonymous rock star. The girls gave us their numbers and told us to make sure we called next time in Houston. We called a taxi and went to the airport sleeping on the way. It was a crazy night.

We flew back to the West Coast and made a couple stops along the way for gas and snacks, mostly along the north side of the border. It was a nice ride and good weather all the way. First stop on the West Coast was Santa Ana Airport to drop John off. He had his dirty white suit on, and he was going to find coke heaven for a few days. He had a few kilos of pot in his suitcase. I was sure I would hear from him when he is broke. Next stop would be my ranch out by Temecula. I was hoping Consuelo would be missing me by now. But I needed to rest for at least a day and night, then off to Hollywood Burbank airport for a night of glitter and fun, then back to the ranch to divide up the weed.

I always had to front the weed to these guys. I get paid most of the time. This kept me from trying to sell it to maybe the cops. I was sure these brotherhood guys would keep their mouths shut if they get busted. That's worth something.

CHAPTER 7

Terminal Island Life

I started to believe I was actually going to jail for six months or two years as we were crossing the bridge to Terminal Island. I did not like its name. It was terminal for one of the inmates, and it happened right outside my window. I watched the whole thing. It was just like in the movies, only real. Several guys gathered around the inmate, and several arms and shiny objects were flying around, and they kept leaning over lower and lower as the inmate kept going down and trying to fight for his life, and then I could see all the blood and one guy was left on the ground. And the killers just wiped off their knives and walked away. Several other inmates were standing with me. We all saw it all, and I immediately forgot what everybody saw. Nobody ever came around asking if anybody saw anything, not any news about it from inside anyway.

Nothing happened for a little while. Then two guards came and picked up the body and took it away, and a little while later, a couple of guys came up with mops and buckets and cleaned it up. And I was standing there, thinking, probably with my mouth open, some large investigation. I knew before a came here that several gangs from San Pedro and Tijuana run the place. I have done favors, and business with some of them outside. Southern California is a small place in some industries. I never had anything to do with hard drugs, and that's their game. So I think they think I was no threat to them, but be very careful about selling anything in Terminal Island.

Terminal Island is a county club-type Federal prison with male and female inmates. It had good food every day and nice feeding hours, as well as activities, such as golf, softball, tennis, and weightlifting. After I walked in, everybody seemed fairly nice. I was searched and given a prison outfit. It was an on-piece prison suit. When you log into a prison on your paperwork, it said income tax evasion, and somehow, they treat those inmates a little better than say armed bank robbery with pistol whipping. I was placed in a cell just like in a police station, nothing but a cot sinks and toilet. I was in there for one week; everybody does that. They do that to see if we were strung out and/or mental or both before we go into the prison population. After seven days, I was sent to the cell block. I walked out with another inmate, and we were to walk across the yard to a certain door and check in and find our cots. He and I decided to walk around the yard a couple of times. First it was so nice to be outside. My first time in the main yard, and I was in violation of the dress code. It turned out you were not allowed to walk the yard in the one-piece prison suit. So I received a small scolding by a prison guard and direction to where we should be.

It was just like the Army large rooms about thirty inmates—bunk beds, polished floors, and very clean restrooms and showers. I was getting set up with my bunk bed on top, and a couple guys walked up and said, "You a pilot?"

I said, "Maybe."

They said, "We knew you were coming." Another So. Cal. friend had told them about me. He was there before me. They said if I need anything let them know, and one of them was a cook in the kitchen. I thought, *This is cool. Now I know people.* And people would know I was not a cop because I had outside connections. But I could not smoke anything until I would get tested here. I think that's what these guys were talking about—smoke and food. I could get any food I wanted delivered to my cot. When they said if I needed anything let them know, it felt good to not be alone here.

This was a fairly relaxed condition about everything. Just do not get in the way of the wrong people, but I have better luck not getting in the way of anyone. It did not take long for me to find the hottest chick in here. Her name was Gloria. She was a smoking hot Latina. She was built and looked like Salma Hayek. I was not sure who she belonged to or if she had a friend with privileges. So I had to be very careful because I did not want to be the main event at a Sushi Show.

The next day, I got to meet my councillor. He was a very cool guy. We got along well. I was sure he doesn't get IRS offenders every day. He asked me what I did for a living. I told him that I was a carpenter and contractor, that I built many houses and apartments. I told him why I was here—my so-called offense. But I did not tell him about my other profession.

Because of my construction experience, he put me in charge of a construction crew. He said we have a large building. We were building it out to have more prison rooms like the one I was living in. It's mostly lay out framing with steel studs and a lot of drywall work. I checked in at the building the next morning. It was right off the main exercise yard. There were six inmates with all kinds of skills, none of them in construction but all good guys willing to learn. Just wait till they would find out they would get free grass. Also there were two guys there with gray suits like work suits. They were not guards. They were overseers of all the construction work around the prison. They were real cool guys. One would be my supervisor. He was young like me, and the older guy was his boss. We talked about different construction projects I had done and seemed to be very happy. I was going to be working there.

After I started working with the crew, my supervisor could see we were really kicking ass and making good progress, and he was coming by less and less; he had other projects. After a while, he only came once a week. When I was close to discharge, the older supervisor stopped by and said that we had done more work for the six months I was there than the other crew took three years to do. The crew that I had all wanted to learn a trade, and they worked very hard and learned enough to carry on and get a job in the trades when they were released. The framing of steel is, of course, fire-proof construction plus a few more benefits. I learned how to frame with steel studs and steel channels when I contracted for a school addition job in Bullhead City, Arizona, a few years ago. Laying out is the hardest part. After that is done, you have a screw gun and screws. Then you screw it all together. After you add the drywall, you have a sturdy wall. It is all very basic, but once you can do this task, it is easy to move on to a higher more skilled task. The next job is hanging Sheetrock. The only thing scary with that is that the inmates have to use razor knifes to cut the board. I have to keep my eyes on those, but none of my guys were violent I hope. The next task was taping all the seams, corners, and screws. But working on all these things every day had made them construction workers with skills. The six months I was there, I trained ten inmates to be good construction workers with a better future. They all watched me real close. They did not want anything to happen to me. That was another reason they liked me so much and loved being on my crew.

The gray suits did not know what was in the ceilings and why it was so popular to work on my crew. You have to be very careful selling anything in Terminal Island. It's in the port of San Pedro docks area. This place was controlled by different factions of the Mexican mafia, the gangs of east Los Angeles, Watts, and San Pedro. However if you cut them in and be careful who you sell to, they would keep you safe from the other gangs here. They were all living mostly comfortably, but there was a lot I did not know or even want to know about what went on inside these walls. The one thing I learned was that they did not investigate murders here, which told me it must not be a big deal, so I better keep a good relationship with all the so-called leaders inside here.

On the last day, I worked out in the area used for weight training. There were four guys standing around an inmate sitting on a lifting bench. Then one of the inmates standing reached over and grabbed a solid steel bar that you load round lifting weights on for the bench press. Anyway, this guy hauled of like a baseball bat swing and nailed this poor inmate on the side of his head and blood spattered everywhere. I went back to my bunk and read a book for a while. I trained there for about a month and could bench press almost three hundred pounds, and after seeing this little incident, I decided maybe exercising here wasn't that healthy and I never went back. I did walk by it the next day. Everybody was working out, and the blood was gone. I never did see that inmate that got cracked on the head around anymore also. I never heard if anybody died around Terminal Island that week. I think when someone is killed, they just write it down in a book somewhere. Life is cheap. I believe in signs, and if that was one, I got it.

My attorneys told me at my trial that they would drug test me sometime while I was inside Terminal Island and to make sure that I stayed out of weed until I was tested. This was important because I did not want to become a hardened prisoner I wanted to be a hardened lover of women. I had to get away from this thing. It's a pretty easy choice—smoke or do eighteen more months.

One day, I was called to the councillor's office. The councillor told me that I had to go to a certain restroom, and they would give me a test. They probably never tested an inmate that was so happy to be tested. I ran upstairs to the specified restroom and walked into the room breathing a tiny bit hard. It was all taped off with a nurse and guard inside. They directed me to a commode, and I took the test and put it in a jar, what was this society turning into. After I took the test, I did not want to go back to work. I thought I would go back to my bunk and celebrate. Now I could bring in some smoke. When I arrived at my bunk area, there were a couple guards standing there. They told me that they found some heroin tucked into the underside of my mattress. I laughed and said, "The guy that lives under me is a junky, and why would I put it there anyway! I was just drug tested." They said they knew that and were waiting for my results. Here I was if my test came back positive, they would be there to take me to where they take the bad boys. But I know that I was clean and thinking about what I was going to do. If they tested me again, I could give them a harassment suitcase, so now I could loosen up some and be me.

The junky that lived below me tested positive for heroin, and I was clean and resolved of any violations of the prison laws. This is not the first time I have had disagreements with this inmate that lived below me. He wanted to be in charge of our little area. He started giving me shit about stepping on his bed to get up to mine. There were a couple inmates in my area standing and talking, and all went silent when I walked up, so I knew they were talking about me. I kept moving forward, and the junky just stood there in front of me, blocking me from my bunk, and I used my two hundred pounds of inertia that I had going and pushed him as hard as I could on the center of his breastplate, which knocked the breath out of him and took him off his feet. He flew back and knocked over the inmate nearest him. They both went down hard. I think he was waiting for me to swing. I put my foot in the middle of his bed and jumped up to mine. The chaos below me silently moved off somewhere. After that, I did not see the junky inmate often. After this incident, everybody knew that I would stand up for myself, and I wasn't a punk.

I was friendly with some of the guys in the San Pedro Gang. Some of them worked with me remodeling the barracks. Some were my Orange County brothers. The San Pedro Gang was one of the biggest dealers here and was local. Things always worked out for the good. If I wanted to know how to get pot in here, they would have to know. I got to know them fairly well and purchased some stank weed a couple of times. We smoked it inside the building we were remodeling. We even had large fans we could blow the smoke out to sea if we wanted. We all smoked cigarettes, and that also covered the smell of marijuana smoke. One day, I asked the oldest one of my crew how I could get some weed in here. He said, "I cannot tell you how, but I can tell you what it cost." So he said the charge was half of whatever they brought in. I thought that sounded like a good deal to me, and I didn't care how it got inside at the time. Then they told me to have someone bring it to Terminal Island. They have a park there for the Coast Guard and their families and place it in this easy-to-find trash can in the park, and the hard part was driving it through the checkpoint. They gave me a couple of ideas how to get it through the checkpoint.

Next thing is to contact my wife. I could not talk on the phone about this. I asked her to come on visiting day. She would come once or twice a month and bring our kids. This time, I wanted to talk to her about the weed. She came the next visiting day. She and the kids all dressed to the nines as always. They look as if they shouldn't be here. I told her to call one of my brothers she knew that usually had a few kilos laying around and tell him I needed one. I have fronted this guy thousands of pounds of weed before, and I was sure he would give her whatever she wanted. Then I told her to pick it up. Then I told her to call a couple of brothers from Anaheim, give them the weed, and tell them what trash barrel in the Coast Guard Private Park on Terminal Island to place it in. The Coast Guard had a club on Terminal Island for Navy and the Coast Guard men and women. To get on Terminal, you have to go through a guard station on the bridge. I told her to tell them to get their hair cut short and get a new car and dress and try to look like young Coast Guard sailors, going out to the club for a few drinks and to have a few beers before they go through the checkpoint. The word was that they never stopped anyone if you looked like you should be there. They drove right through checkpoint with armed Coast Guard Military Police. They found and placed the kilo in the rite trash can.

The next morning, the outside landscaping crew went out to clean and mow the Island Park and happened by the trash can, grabbed the kilo, and placed it inside the lawn mower. After they finished their day, they drove it through the prison gates. Then they drove it up to the door of the building I was working on and carried it in, and we cut it in half. I guess I knew how they got it in now. My crew helped me put it in the ceiling after we all took out a small stash. We made a secret spot for it, put it in the ceiling, and covered it up with some drywall.

And then we waited for a few hours and then started smoking. The weed can be traded or sold. I did not want to start competing with the gangs, so most of it I gave away, and with all my crew smoking, I didn't really have any to sell. Most of my friends were from Orange County. Life was good now. Pot could even be traded for sex. I wasn't interested in that. I only had a few months left, and I didn't want to leave here with anything I didn't come in here with. Terminal Island had girls. The most famous one was one of the Manson girls. She had a swastika scar on her forehead, which was fairly easy to see. It's not very attractive to me. I always tried not to make eye contact with her. She was looking at me a lot. There were a few nice ones there. One of them threw a hamburger at me one time in the mess hall, but that's a whole other thing.

Everyone said, "Do not make friends in prison," and I took that advice except for J Dub. He was cool and dealt in small amounts of pot. His girlfriend smuggled the pot into the prison. I think that's how she made her living. He was visited by her often. He was from Vancouver, Canada, and had connections at the Flabob Airport in Riverside, California. That was where I was checked out in flying the twin Beech. I was very familiar with it. I have been there more times than you can count, by highway and/or by airways.

After J Dub got out, we started a business. I furnished the weed, and he took it to Canada and sold it. I had lived in Solana Beach on the side of a hill overlooking the ocean with a large camper in the driveway that could not be seen from the street. It would usually have five hundred pounds to one thousand pounds of weed in it most of the time. I opened a small flight service at a Southern California Airport. I owned several airplanes and had some on lease back. That I could use anytime. Jay had a pilot, and he would fly the weed he purchased, take it to Canada, and bring me back more money. I traveled up there the first time to make sure I received the rest of the money, but I know now he would send the money to me.

This could be a long story, but they got stopped flying back south in a small plane with some cash money, $79,000. They stopped for gas at a noncontrolled airport, and the cops stopped them, and they didn't look like they should be there and ask a few questions. The Canadians had worked around me somehow and had found another Mexican dealer, so he lost the Mexicans money, not mine. What I still think about was when we needed to get money exchanged, we went to the large international airport, and in the large waiting areas with hundreds of people, he would meet a guy and hand him a paper bag with $50,000 Canadian money. The guy walked off, and we had a beer or two, and their beer knocked me on my butt. Soon the guy returned and handed the bag that now had American money in it. Jimmy said, "Don't worry about it. We can count it in the car, but it will be right." Jimmy must really be connected to have friends in the money exchange business at the airport that he can trust with that kind of money like it's no big deal.

I met this guy in a Federal prison, and I was standing here with $50,000. Now I had to drive back across the border and then fly my plane back to California. Then they faded out for a while. After about ten years later, Jimmy contacted me and said they owned a nursery in British Columbia and were growing some very strong buds. When could I come up and see him? And how much did I want? I wasn't doing much at the time and took a flight to Seattle. He had his secretary pick me up at the airport.

Desera is smoking hot with dark brown soft hair and turquoise blue eyes with hourglass the whole nine yards. Anyway we were driving up to the Canadian border, and it's around dinnertime. I said I was hungry, and she must be too, so I said, "Let's stop for dinner." I was looking down at the city from a freeway overpass, and I saw this tower, the Seattle Space Needle that had a restaurant spinning on top, and I say, "Let's go there." And she was a little excited and said she had never been and would love to go. She took the next turnoff the highway and headed toward the tower. She was very nice, and wow, all these girls would love a green card. I felt very good with surf and turf with Captain Morgan and coke. We must have spent at least an extra four or five hours on a two-hour trip.

Jimmy must have been going nuts, but he didn't have to. There was nothing going on but eating, socializing, and traveling in style This little babe was wild, but anyway, by the time we arrived, Jimmy had gone to the hospital with a possible drug overdose. I didn't see him till the next day in the hospital, and I told him I was sorry it took so long for the drive from Seattle to Vancouver, but I was starving and did not like airline food. I had to stop. Jimmy said he talked to his girlfriend, and she said she had a good time. Then Jimmy said I could pick up some smoke in Santa Cruz, California, at his friend's house. He gave me his friend's address and number, as well as a name and address to send the money to in Canada. Send or bring the money back. That's how it started the second time. This was ten years later, and after that was over, I received an official letter from the Royal Canadian Mounties addressed to me that basically said if I never come back to Canada that we won't look for you. I have no idea how they could have my address; Jimmy didn't even have it. But now I need to get a job in the airline industries, and I have built up enough flight hours to qualify for a job with an airline company that flew turbine engine airplanes. The next time I went to Canada a few years later, it was on an airline flight, and I was the captain, and when I went through customs, they never blinked, but they all took a good look at me. All the international airports had a customs line that said Crew Only for the pilots. One late night at Montreal Airport, there was no one there at the Customs station we just walked through. I even took Squeaky John to Toronto with me one night during a blizzard. We were flying films for Time Life Corporation. I would fly for them when the weather got so bad and they could not send the photo signals to the printers, for their magazines.

My sentence was reduced to six months for good behavior, just as my attorneys were telling me. George, my attorney, turned out to be a personal friend over the years. The first time I saw his image, he was on the front page of the Santa Ana Register holding his head, during the Timothy Leary Trial. Sometime later I was arrested for DUI after the over one-hundred-dred-mile-an-hour chase, two counties. I contacted George and told him I had to beat this case no matter what it cost. I wanted to be an airline pilot, and the DUI would put me out of a chance to get hired. And I asked him to handle the case. The DUI had to be handled in another county. It was late at night, and chase lasted a little long I had a new Thunderbird. George hired a lawyer from the other county to help out. He knew the judge. The charge was changed to reckless driving. The attorney explained to the judge that I could not have been drunk if I could drive that fast and not crash at driving over one hundred miles an hour. The arresting officers did not attend. They must have been blown away if they saw the trial results. They had to help me stand up to walk over to their cars when they arrested me and dropped to reckless driving. Then a briefcase was left at George's office full of money.

The arresting officer told me to blow in this thing, and I was leaning on my car, so I could stand up. I said, "If I blow, you going to take me to jail."

He said, "We are going to jail anyway". I did not blow; that was the evidence they needed. My dad taught me that trick. If you ever get pulled over, do not blow. The bottom line for not blowing is that I would lose my driver's license for a year. I never went to the trial. Nobody ever told me anything about or ever ask me to send in my license. It would probably be in the highway patrol computer system. The word around the brothers was that you could get a picture driver's license in New Mexico easy.

So the next day after the trial, I flew my bonanza to Albuquerque New Mexico, rented a car, and stopped at a motel and picked up a card for their address for my driver's license application and proceeded to the motor vehicle department. I filled out all the paperwork and was issued a nice new picture driver's license. I think it was thirty-five bucks, but I was good to go now. I flew back to California and got in late. My instrument lights went out on the way. There was a moon, so I could see the mountains. I had good weather. I had a matchbook full of matches. I used the last one to see my airspeed on final approach into the Santa Ana Airport. Twenty-year-old airplanes always have little problems.

George invited me over to his New Year's party. I had no idea he would invite Romain and Purcell, two narcs from Laguna. There were lots of attorneys and judges, doctors, and educators; also some of the Newport beach high society was there. I was sure they all could see my car, a brand-new four-door Thunderbird with the suicide rear doors. I had been drinking before I arrived and could see no parking spots except for George's front yard. That made it easy for the narcs to get my license plate number. I had a Pat Boone outfit: white silk turtleneck shirt, blue sport coat on khakis, white leather sneakers, shoulder-length hair, and all. There were plenty of people there all dressed up, drinking, getting a little friendly and loud. After I had a drink and moved around, I did not know anyone but George's wife, Sharon, who was a good friend of mine. We have all gone on road trips to Hollywood together. One time we missed the turn off and wound up in the desert. With me were Cathy and Marty, George, and Sharon. After I located her, we hugged and friendly kissed. We talked for a while. Then I saw George, and he invited me into his office and showed me some of the new things he had. We checked them out and then I told him I would be on the way as it was late and I had a drive ahead of me and I wanted to stop by Finnigan's Rainbow Room in Newport Beach on the way home.

The day before I was discharged from Terminal Island, we had a party in my bunk area. It was something done to many inmates when they get discharged. They discharge early in the morning, so people have time to get to their halfway house. Notice I didn't say inmates. The big deal in California prisons is we that have avocadoes for every party treat, Christmas, birthdays, and Fourth of July. Good for me because one of my besties was a cook from Orange County. He had free rein of the kitchen. Did I say this is a Country Club Correction Center?

It corrected me. I would never not pay my income tax. I was thinking as my wife picked me up in her new Chevrolet metallic blue Monte Carlo with the big block engine. We were driving back to Cardiff-by-the-Sea so I could gather my things and my El Camino. It had a fiberglass camper shell and held exactly five hundred pounds. It had made plenty of trips to the city. In California slang, that means Frisco. Now it held everything I had after losing my ranch to the revenuers. Now I was going to my safety deposit box and picked up some cash and then went see my friend in Laguna and picked up some needed items.

Next stop was my halfway house on Kerny Mesa. As I walked into the front door, standing there was an old friend of mine. He was a carpenter and worked for me for several years. He was working with my friends from San Diego North County. doing what I was doing, only he got caught. He spent some time in Lompoc Federal prison where the poor people go. It was nice to have someone I know there. I was there for only a couple days. I told the halfway house manager that I was a contractor and could support myself. I was given the name of a parole officer and a few days to contact him.

My Fastest Little Twin

After that, I leased a half of a duplex in a canyon in Cardiff-by-the-Sea. I started a flying business at the local airport, purchased a new airplane, and began to pay my income taxes, and the story goes on.

CHAPTER 8

Thai Sticks to New York

Chuck stopped over one morning. He moved down to North County along with Jack and Bart, near me after I was released from incarceration. North County was cool. None of the little towns along the coast had their own police forces. Law enforcement was handled by the county sheriffs. They seemed to be cool, and they didn't have any overzealous officers like some of the other beach communities. Chuck asked me if I would be interested in taking a plane load of Thai Stix to New York City. At the time, my largest airplane was a Cessna 402. It was a twin-engine cabin-class unpressurized airplane. I had it on a lease back from William. It was based at Flabob Airport in Riverside, California. I usually kept it at the beach airport near my house. Chuck asked me If I could do it today. I asked him how long it would take to have it ready.

Then I told him it had to be packaged airtight, and I know he had the equipment to suck out the air and seal the packages, then put it all in suitcases that lock. The lock is important because if asked, I would say I did not have keys and they would have to break into one of the cases, and that would be illegal without a warrant. I wanted it to look like nothing but luggage. This way, if I ever get asked about my freight, I had a pad of manifest forms from a freight airline. I would say, "This is airline baggage loaded on a wrong plane, and we are repositioning it."

Chuck, Keith, and I met up at Flabob Airport in Riverside, California. It had a sheriff's office on the road to the airport. You have to drive by it to get to the airport. Most people were afraid to do nefarious things around any airport because the police were close by. Most people would not bring drugs around the sheriffs there, and that made it nice. If people did not have purpose there, they could have a problem. There were places on Flabob Field between the hangers that you can load or off-load an airplane and not raise any eyebrows. Chuck and Keith, a friend of mine from high school in Anaheim, had a truck. Chuck said I could use Keith to help me with the trip, and I said this was good a familiar face. Keith was ready to go and happy to come along. One of my girlfriends would ride with us also.

Everything was loaded, tanks were full, and we were ready to take off. I made a call to the flight service station and got the weather for Albuquerque. It would be my first stop. The weather was visual flight rules now, but my estimated time of arrival was forecast to be instrument flight rules. There was an airport near Albuquerque that I know was laid back a few miles north of town and had good clean fuel. The weather was hard to track as weather radar was at its infancy at the time. It was wintertime now, and I know there would be snow and ice along the way.

I know there were some storms brewing around the center of the USA. I would have to dodge or go around it as I was not pressurized and could not get above the ice. If I have to go around the storm, I would have to go around it to the north because if I go south, I would be near the border and could be looking like a smuggler from Mexico. I would stay way north of it. The Cessna 402 is equipped with anti-ice and deice equipment, but it was all old stuff and probably didn't work. It is basically a California airplane and never flies on the ice like the pilot.

We took off, and I turned off all my radios. I know the way to Albuquerque without navigation equipment. I turned the transponder off and anything that made a radio wave. We were in the dark mode now. If we were being watched or chased, we could not be found. We were on the way and passing over Arizona, and now we were in New Mexico over some mountains, and we were in a snowstorm, and the visibility was deteriorating. At least, it was really cold now, and the snow was not sticking to the airplane. It was starting to get dark, and we were also low on fuel. I needed to find an airport soon, so I was going over my charts and looking for the closest one with fuel. The good thing is that we passed the Sandia Mountains. We would be mostly over flatlands now.

We found a gold mine of an airport somewhere in Northern New Mexico or southern Colorado. The state lines on these air charts were hard to see—a Ma and Pa airport out in the middle of nowhere. They were so happy to see us. They knew we would buy lots of fuel. They put our airplane in their hanger for the night as we were in a blowing snowstorm that was moving northeast like us. We would let it pass during the night and try again tomorrow.

We borrowed the airport car and went to a motel and spent the night. I was a little worried after we left the airport that they might look into my airplane. The reason was that the doors did not lock. Most of these old freight airplanes had doors that did not lock, and most freight pilots knew that. If you know how to start them and fly them, you probably would not steal one. It does not take a key to start like little planes, just a toggle switch that said power on or off. Not rocket science—only keys for the doors. I liked the airport people and got a good vibe from them.

We had our skis and boots and things on top of the luggage. If they looked inside, it would look like we had been snow skiing, and the lady who was pretty and tall who could be a model had a lot of luggage. I did not think they would mess with our airplane. When we showed up the next morning, I was glad not to see any cop cars around the airport. We fueled the airplane, and I drew a circle around the airport on my chart to save it as a good fuel stop coming out of Mexico some other time.

We took off and started northeast to the Denver area. We could see the bad weather east of us. We were cruising at nine thousand feet, heading northeast. I was trying to head more east, but the weather over there was getting worse, driving me farther and farther north. After a few hours, we were in Sioux Falls, South Dakota, and we wanted to be in Saint Louis. We were in the middle of a blizzard and low on fuel and way north of our route. I decided to make an instrument approach in Sioux Falls, South Dakota. It was well below zero there, high winds from the northeast, fifty knots gusting to sixty knots. The sky condition was two hundred overcast in blowing snow, which was not normal for this southern California crew.

As we were starting our descent, I noticed that some of the engine controls were harder and harder to operate. The one that bothered me most was the mixture controls as the mixture was leaned out as we climbed to maintain proper fuel-air mixture as we climb. The air was thinner up. Higher you need less fuel, which increases fuel range. I needed to get the mixture controls to full rich when we got near the ground, or the engines would quit. I was forcing the mixture knobs full forward, and I was afraid the cables were frozen due to all the moisture I have been flying through and the extremely cold wet weather.

Now I was descending through four thousand, and the left engine mixture lever was full forward full rich. Right engine mixture was in the halfway forward position, and the right engine was starting to run a little rough. I needed to fix this mixture that must be full rich, or the engine would flame out. I slid my captain's chair full aft and put my right foot on the engine control pedestal and pushed forward using my leg muscle, and then the cable just snapped, and the mixture lever went all the way forward. My eyes went immediately to the fuel flow gauge, and the fuel flow had not changed, so I know the cable broke.

Bad news, I added a little more power on the good engine as I did not want to get distracted and let my airspeed decrees below VMC. Fortunately, I had my speed way up to contend with the high winds. If I had to use differential power to straighten the airplane out just before touchdown, it wouldn't be there, and the runway was covered with snow and ice. I know it would be slippery and there was no braking report available as the weather was too bad. There was no other traffic or traffic scheduled because of the poor weather. I know it would take full aileron into the wind on touchdown to go straight down the runway. Now I was real low and it was dark, and I saw the approach lighting system. A moment later, I saw the runway lights and the runway. The right engine quit, just as we touched down.

I had the ground control direct me to the largest open FBO and keep the plane rolling and moving so I could taxi in on one engine. I pulled into the ramp area in front of the flight office. We unloaded ourselves and walked into the warm office. The lady at the counter asked what she could do for me. I said I had a broke airplane and needed maintenance. She called the maintenance supervisor. He walked into the office, and I explained the problem. He agreed with me that the mixture cable was probably broken. We were so far north of the border. Nobody would suspect that the plane was loaded with pot. So I helped them tow the airplane to the hanger and wait for the report.

The maintenance pros pulled the cowling off and reported that as suspected, the cable was broken and it would take a couple of weeks to have a replacement sent. They would be expecting us in New York the next night. So I decided we would rent three cars and drive the Stix the rest of the way. I told Keith we would not check in with Chuck till we would get to New York in case there was a phone line tap. If we drove straight through, we could make it.

I have my American Express card. The weather is so bad this is like a Ghost town around the airport. I rent the Cars, and I know how to open large Hanger Doors. We take the three cars into the hanger and fill the back seats and trunks with the suitcases and start driving. Everyone was following a couple of cars back its freeways all the way. I estimated about twenty to twenty-four hours for the trip. I think it snowed all the way to Cleveland. We just cruised along. We saw no accidents. It was all smooth driving Highway 80. My girlfriend and I had warm clothes, and we were going to Ski Powder in Aspin on our return trip. When we called Chuck after we arrived in New York City, he directed us to a duplex in uptown Manhattan.

We found out later that night by an informant we had that the police were expecting the shipment and had all the metropolitan airports staked out for twenty-four hours for three days and nights waiting for us. When we showed up in Manhattan in cars, that really threw them off. It was getting late, and we were finally settling down in the duplex when the doorbell rang. I looked out the peephole, and I could see two guys with a tool bag kind of dirty looking and moved back into the room. They rang a few more times and then started breaking into the steel door.

They were having no luck with simple hand tools. The steel door was twelve inches thick and had a heavy steel door jamb; the concrete walls were about two feet thick. They didn't have enough tools to break in and finally gave up. I looked out the window as they were exiting the door below and saw them with their tool bag, not issued by the department I suspect. I looked around from the second-story window where I was calling out for police and saw no policeman around. There was always one on one of the corners. I yelled out that I was going to call the police. One of them cried out over his shoulder as they ran around the corner carrying their tool bags and a crowbar, "We are the police."

I called Chuck, and he said we should go to a hotel and call him. We checked into a nice hotel just around the corner, and we just went to sleep. We had been up for days. The next day, I had to turn the cars in to stop the charges. It turned out I lost money on this trip. Chuck turned in one of them and said one was stolen. Ha, maybe on the way to Texas. The next day, I went to the rental car company and told them the car was stolen. I have insurance on everything, so I wasn't worried about having to pay for it. Then they gave me a piece of paper to take to the port authority car storage lot and have them sign it, saying the car was not there. And so, it was another trip into the belly of traffic. We arrived there and showed our paperwork after waiting in line, while people were paying their parking fines and driving away in their ransomed cars. The lady went through all their information and signed the paper saying that the rental car was not in their lot. We went directly to the airport and turned in my rental car and the paperwork on the stolen one. They handed me some papers to sign and keep. The next thing was direct to LAX. We arrived in the evening, and I had one of my pilots pick us up at LAX and fly us down to the beach airport. Chuck called me when he returned and told me where to go to pick up the twenty-five pounds I charged for the trip. I went to a house in Fountain Valley and picked up a suitcase, with the pot in it. I drove it home. After I arrived, I wanted to smoke some and opened some of it up. It seemed fine at first, but after I looked at it, it was decided that most of the sticks were water leaves tied around the sticks to look like buds. I ended up throwing about half of it away. I couldn't be real mad. These guys have kept me in Afghani hash and brought me mucho dinero for tons of weed. Now I had to go back to Winter Wonderland, Sioux Falls, South Dakota, and retrieve my airplane and pay for the repairs.

A few days later, I met Chuck at my ranch in Valley Center, and we talked about the trip to New York. He was telling me that the owner of the duplex where it was in Manhattan was from a large banking family and said there were millions of dollars' worth of antiquities and artifacts that he had gathered around the world. He also said the owner emptied out the duplex the next morning, and the cops came back the next night with sledgehammers and a grinder and broke into the empty duplex. He also said the cops were tipped off that we were coming to town with a thousand pounds of Thai sticks, and they also knew about the duplex and that I would be there. He had more inside information. He said the cops that were looking for us were famous for asking questions over a toilet bowl and were really pissed because they had to stay up day and night staking out the airports for three days and nights. And we arrived in cars. I could sense that they were pissed when that guy in Manhattan yelled. We were the police running away from the duplex. Probably he was tired, and his shift was changing, and he knew the pot was here somewhere in the city. He got beat, and I got away again because the airplane froze and broke. It was luck or divine intervention, probably more like luck.

When Chuck came over to hire me to fly the Stixs to Manhattan, it wasn't a complete surprise to me. He hired me to fly up north to look, to see if the Coast Guard cutters were in their respective ports on a certain day. I think Jack came over and picked me up and said we were going to Laguna Beach to see about a job. On the way, we picked up Chuck in Jack's Green Beemer. We had a comfortable ride when we arrived. We pulled into a large house and walked in. There at his desk was Kilo John. I was quite surprised as I had not seen him for several years. The last time I saw him, he came out to my ranch to tell me he lost the 500 kilos I fronted him. At least I got my motor home back. But anyway I did not want to create a scene there, with all his people on his turf. This is all eternal love, right?

He told me he was bringing in a load of Thai Sticks in Northern California. He wanted me to fly over a couple of Coast Guard Stations and see if the cutters were in port. He gave me someone I knew but don't remember who to come with me that had a radio-size backpack I had seen them in the Army with him. He would call the ship and report what we see. This would be worth twenty-five pounds of sticks, he said. That sounded fair to me. I had several airplanes that could do the job. He then called this guy forward that was standing a little bit behind him and said, "This is my captain."

I said, "Nice to meet you." We made some small talk about airplanes. I guess he wanted to make certain that whoever did the observation trip had the right equipment, and he could count on it. And the reason I was driven up to Laguna was that the captain wanted to see before he pulled his ship into the twelve-mile limit. And I mean ship. This thing must have been a couple of hundred feet long and fifty feet wide.

After I made my run up the coast and cleared the area and the radio telephone operator (RTO) for people without Military minds made the all-clear radio call to the ship, I made a wide left turn and went out to sea little to see if I could get a glimpse of the ship, and I did it, which blew my mind. This thing was blowing tons of diesel smoke out its stacks and was going I would bet close to forty knots; the wake would sink most boats. It was like couple hundred feet long and fifty feet wide. A short fat ocean-going fast boat. It was painted in this green-gray radar-absorbing paint. I could not count all the antennas it had on it—some satellite antennas and two or three radar antennas. This had to be some government ship. I was wondering what kind of shit John got us into. Were we working for the CIA now?

I was hoping that Captain did not remember me. He had a visible likeness to a CIA agent I would see on TV. Also, I was thinking I better get my ass out of here. He must have something for defense. My airplane was white with red and blue stripes. I immediately showed him the tail of my airplane. This area was very dense, that there was not much going on up here close to the Oregon border. There was no air traffic but lots of cold and wind. I was flying a Cessna 182, fairly heavy for a light plane but heavy enough that it did not get tossed around in the heavy gusty winds so much.

The airplane held plenty of fuel, so after we finished spotting, we headed southbound and got several hundred miles south before we stopped for fuel so we could make the rest of the way home.

Several days later, an old friend of mine who lived in the desert called me with a proposition for some flight time. He said he had a friend that rented a Grand Banks motor yacht to do a trip to Mexico and bring back some weed. The rental company somehow found out they were smugglers and alerted the Coast Guard. There was a group of California smugglers that had a small syndicate that was a really unorganized crime. The other guys tried to connect us through the organized crime lane called RICO. But it was a joke.

Her husband was planning to land the Grand Banks somewhere near the Channel Islands in Northern California. I have been there in my ketch and by air. I was familiar with the area. If you see travel films of Italy and Greece, we had the same thing right here off the California coast although a little cooler. There is one island in the chain of islands with a cavern that I could power into with my ketch. The ceiling must be a hundred feet high. My main mast was sixty feet high, and I could still maneuver around. We had no bow thrusters then, and we did not need them. It was unbelievable—the calm of the water and winds inside the island.

We have a small group of smugglers in California. It's a small world as they say. She told me how she had heard about me and wanted me to fly out and find them in the Grand Banks and drop a bottle with a note in it telling them that the Coast Guard was alerted and looking for them. The next thing was finding a wine bottle, pen and paper, and an airplane that had a window that opened in flight. I had three. I wanted a slow one so I could get to know this young lady in a thin cotton dress. We drove out to the airport. I had to stop and pick up my go bag. She had a small suitcase with her, and we drove out to the airport. We found a wine bottle on the way with a cork, and she made a note that said the Coast Guard was looking for them. She said they would be around the Channel Islands by Monterey, California, any day now or within the next couple of days, depending on the winds and currents.

We started out going north toward Santa Catalina Island and swooped down low as we go over Avalon and the Yacht Harbor where I have been many times, only this time a little above sea level. I mean any red-blooded man would want to show off a little but still get the job done. We would fly around the area between the Coronado Islands, Catalina Island, and the Channel Island Chain, covering a three-hundred-mile area till we start getting low on fuel. I figure with the speed of their boat, it would take ten or twelve hours to move into that area we just searched. So we can take a twelve-hour break till we need to go back out. So we decided to go to Santa Barbara for the night. She was a little low-budget but very high class, so she said we had to get one room in the hotel. I wish I could have had my Apple watch to check my blood pressure, at that moment. The next morning, we woke up and had breakfast, bought some snacks, filled up the tanks with 100 low lead fuel, and headed out to sea.

Every day, we went a little further out to sea, and it became about a hundred miles further than glide distance. We did not have a raft or life jackets; I just don't think it's not my time to go. We flew out in the morning and flew for two or three hours, then came back, and landed for lunch. We waited for a couple of hours and flew out till dark. The scenery around the Channel Islands is crazy. Beautiful wildflowers cover some of the large areas.

On the third day we went out, sure enough we spot the Grand Banks chugging along. She was going real slow. This boat was sitting so low in the water. It must have five tons of smoke in it. I had no trouble identifying it as our boat. I changed my course a little as to fly low right over the top of the boat. I told her to open her window and shout at them. As we passed over, I pulled the power to idle on the plane, and she shouted, "Coast Guard." Her head was part way out the window, and with her silky hair blowing all over the place, they had to recognize her. As I started my turn, I looked back over my shoulder and could see four or five guys waving, jumping, and yelling. I circled the boat a couple of times, checking the wind. I wanted to drop the bottle close to the front of the boat, but not hit the boat. We only had one bottle. Maybe we should have brought more bottles.

After I read the winds and the Grand Banks heading, I went out about a half-mile and came back low and slow. Her window was still open it's like riding a Harley at a hundred miles an hour. I told Cynthia to get ready to drop the wine bottle. We were on a direct path to the front of the boat at a ninety-degree angle. I wanted to put it in front of the boat on the port side.

She dropped the bottle on my signal, and it landed near the front of the boat. We circled around the boat and could see the crew netting the bottle and bringing it aboard. We did another lap around the boat, and we saw that they opened the bottle and read the note. We did one more lap around, and I came in over the top super low fast full power full speed, heading for shore. We went back to San Diego. I never saw her again. She was a very nice young lady.

A few months later, I ran into my friend who told me about the job. He said after they picked up the bottle, they went to one of the Channel Islands and unloaded all the weed. While they were doing it at night, the Coast Guard and Marines launched a full-scale assault on the island. They arrested everyone and put them in jail.

I ran into my friend who told me about the job about a year or two later, and he told me Cynthia's husband got out of jail and somehow learned to fly and got an airplane and was coming back across the border over San Diego and was flying real low and hit a highway overpass in the fog. That's when his story ended.

CHAPTER 9

I Found a Gold Mine

This story started with Raymond and TJ coming out to my ranch with a plan for a scam. They wanted me to fly down to Mexico and pick up a load of Weed. This sounds easy to say but there is a lot of planning and if it is not good, I will be the one that suffers most. They tell me Raymond has a friend that owns a Cessna 337 twin-engine airplane, turns out it is the model that is pressurized Turbocharged very fast and the heaviest, not designed for short soft field landings. Now they tell me the landing strip they have is on the top of a mountain in Sinaloa and is used for a Gold and opal mine. There are no roads to reach this mine the miners walk and lead pack burrows to get there. They use short-field aircraft for emergencies and to ship gold in the mornings while it is cool.

We looked over all my charts and got a good estimate of flight time. I told them that I would do the job for my usual charge of $50.000 per trip. I was going to bring back around 700 pounds. I would take half my money in weed after I landed in Texas and twenty-five thousand after TJ sold the weed. Bad move on my part. I had been chased out of California by the feds and was living in Pennsylvania by now these Scams take a few months sometimes. Needless to say, it would be hard to pick up my $25.000. Raymond was my best friend he was a licensed real Estate Broker, he taught me if one is good two are better. He bought and sold several homes for me, and I trusted him a lot because he has handled large amounts of cash in the past more than $25.000 and he always paid me.

The first thing on my list was secure the aircraft meet the owner and get the keys. This guy was so rich he lived on an estate in Rancho Santa Fe if you do not know where that is you can ask any San Diego attorney or King. He had another house or estate in Palm Springs and that is where the Cessna is based at. I will call him Dave he was Raymond's friend I called him and ask him to meet me at LAX airport FBO so I could pick up the Airplane. I would be coming in from Ohio at 8 PM. After I landed, I called the LAX Flight Business Office for a car to take me from the Airline side to the private side of the airport to the Flight Business Office.

When I walked in I was met by Dave and his wife what a babe They were an extremely nice couple and ask me if I would fly them to San Diego in their plane, spend the night in their home, and then fly them to Palm Springs the next day. Then, I could take the airplane back to PA and learn how to fly it well. This is a very fast 220 KTS at FL 200 which is good for long distances, but not for low-level flying under the radar. The airplane is heavy pressurized and is designed for nice long paved runways. The runway I was going to was maybe 1500 feet on a high mountain with thin air. This airplane needed more than that for take-off and landing. Sometimes I can land and take off short by using some advanced techniques but very tricky for heavy airplanes that do not bounce.

Spending a couple of days with Dave we talked about the airplane I said it is not a good idea to use this plane. Finally, I said do you want me to give you a demonstration and he said yes. So, I told him we will take off in the morning and fly down to the strip on the mountain in Mexico and try to land, if we can land check out the strip and then fly back to Texas. There would not be enough fuel to fly back to California. Then we would return to Cali the next day. I guess it would be a great adventure for them. We would not have any drugs with us so if we were intercepted and not shot down, I could say my navigation equipment failed. My PO would probably never find out about it. I think back about my arraignment the judge said That I would have to surrender my pilot's license, and passport and I could not leave the state. My attorney jumped up and said he needs his license for his job and he leaves the state sometimes every day. I am laughing to myself my job is to fly weed, as the judge says he can keep his pilot license and leave the state but not the country.

We drove out to the Palm Springs Airport the next morning with overnight bags and some sandwiches and soft drinks. I planned to fly down to the mountains east of Torreon which TJ pointed out to me on a map. I would be able to land on the strip look it over and check it out and water a tree. Then we would fly over a few more mountains and land in Texas this airplane had four large tanks and could fly for 7 hours. We will land in Texas for fuel and to spend the night. On the trip, I would check out this other landing strip on the way that I have used before. It was in the right area a large valley with a big landing strip in it nobody around for a hundred miles. I can use it if I have any problems or emergencies.

The trip was great for me because I would be able to prove my judgement to Dave about his airplane for the flight. I would see the landing I am supposed to land on, and if I can land on it. On the way, I will check out other runways I have used in the past. Also, everything would be paid for by Dave and I would just spend a couple of days and learn a lot. He had a private pilot license and could fly a little I think Raymond said he was a Chemist. We took turns flying I did the navigating, and the wife was in the back handing us drinks and sandwiches. Palm springs is a good place to leave from it is in the Desert. I ask the tower for an east departure and was given it so I flew east at 9,000 feet for about a hundred miles and dropped down to a hundred feet and turned south and crossed the border. After leaving California at a low level over the desert, then we climbed to 18,000 and it was just a smooth ride for a few hours. I was triangulating between three radio beacons. To find the position of the mountain with the strip. I was at seventeen thousand and radar out here was a joke. I would stay up high for a low fuel burn with a slow descent until I see the strip then just spiral down to it and slow all the time to be at ten knots above stall speed which is fairly fast at these altitudes on short final. And I never looked at the book so, what it means to me when the wings start shaking like mad you are close to stall speed and you better be adding power or descending.

I can see the runway now we are still a little high and clear blue skies and super weather for this. The top of this mountain is like covered with jungle. These guys carved out this runway on one side of the mountain to get the gold to market without bandits. There is a solid jungle on each end of it and around it. This runway runs uphill one way in and one way out, this is good. As I was configuring the airplane for landing, I was taking all this in. The good thing about the Cessna is it has a high wing so you can see the ground underneath.

As I am getting closer and lower I can see this will not work out but I have to scare the shit out of Dave and his wife so they will understand that this airplane is not right for the job. I am down to the level of the landing strip and at a slow speed, I will fly around the mountain one more time and line up and make an approach to land. I am about five hundred feet from the runway and the stall warning starts to hum and buffet the controls are sluggish and now I am just a few feet from landing and we are already past the middle of the runway. I may have miss judged the density altitude a little, but I never said I was perfect only I will always get you home. So, remember when I said the controls were getting a little sluggish well now they are big-time sluggish. I added full power and full up on the controls the stall warning was screaming and I was trying to accelerate down what little runway was left rather than clime and that with the Turbochargers saved us.

When I got to the end of the runway, I put my feet on the floor and pulled up as hard as I could, and we heard a loud thump it looked like we bounced off the hammock of the jungle now I was heading straight up and I had to push the joke all the way forward to prevent a stall. I used the full range of the airplanes controls to get out of there. We are all shaking I am trying to hide my shaking and act like this is every day flying. It's just my Knees, I think this is why we do this shit. They are silent and didn't say anything for a while. Then when we are in cruise mode, they loosened up a little and said they understood why that plane would not work in Technicolor. They thought they were going to die and could not believe I saved the plane and them. I know I may have damaged their landing gear and should I retract it? If it is damaged it could jamb and cause a crash. I pulled the flaps up and started to set up for the cruise and looking at the mountains and deciding the shortest route to Texas. Now I need to figure out if we could make it to Texas by dragging the landing gear not retracting this means burning more fuel. After a few minutes I decided it would be close with the gear down, so I decided to retract it. The airplane was insured and a gear-up landing would be better than fuel starvation somewhere in the desert. If we had a gear-up landing at least I would have fire equipment at any US airport. Then we landed eventually at a large Texas Airport with no problem. The kid that refuelled the airplane handed me a couple of pieces of a banana leaf and said he found it in my landing gear when he attached the grounding cable.

Dave and his wife decided that he and his wife would be flying airline back to California. They were very impressed with that flight and agreed with me about the right airplane. Then Dave asks what airplane I would want, and I said a near-new 182 RG. He said for me to take the 337 home and I will call you when I have a 182RG for you to pick up. About a week later he called me and said I could keep the Cessna 337 and use it for a while in my charter business until he decided what to do with it. I had a small air Taxi company in a flyover state. He said he would purchase a 182RG and leave it at the FBO at LAX where we met before, and I could pick it up there any time, and Good Luck.

I had a couple of things to get in order and then flew out to LAX the next day. I picked up the airplane after I landed and flew it out to Borrego Hot springs it is a small airport that has a motel on it you park your plane beside your room and is very nice. I have a friend that has a ranch near there if I need anything he will be able to help me. The Airport is rummerd to be a place where Aviators with secretaries and girlfriends can fly out for a Quicky and be back in a city in a couple of hours. I have staged here before it's all flat desert to Mexico. I need water, food and a sleeping bag a hunting knife and to take along for a two-day trip. My rancher brother brought it all that night with ten five-gallon empty gas cans and a ladder. I gave him some hundred-dollar bills and said TJ will give him a kilo when he gets back from Texas. Late that night we filled the gas cans up at the airport it has a gas pump that uses credit cards. We also topped off the 182 with gas.

I have been in contact with Raymond, and he knows I am ready, so I hope he calls tonight. I need to hear from him about what day I will make the pick-up. His Mexican will pack that weed up to the mountain on burros. One reason why I am doing this is to find a landing strip that soldiers will never be at. We will see.

I plan to fly down to the landing strip in the valley first land and pour all the fuel into the wings and then fly up to the mountain strip land and load the weed and fly on to Texas. TJ will meet me at an airport in Texas. I have used it before at night and unloaded the weed. He will then drive the weed to California. I will fly to a close by the airport which means around a hundred miles away in case Tj gets caught. Then spend the night and fly back to California the next day. That's the plan this is how it came down.

I get the call from Raymond that night he says the Mexicans are on the way to the mountain with the weed and will be there in the afternoon. TJ is in Texas and will be there tomorrow night. The Mexicans have been sitting on this weed for almost two weeks so I am pretty sure they will be on time or at least be there. I get a few hours of sleep and take off for Mexico and plan another long day. I do not see another plane on the trip I know almost all the mountain ranges in Northern Mexico, like California and do not need a map until I get close. The Runway in the Valley is easy to find I do I big circle around it to see if anyone is around about twenty miles and it's all clear, so I land. I unload the cans and the ladder and pour the gas into the fuel tanks in each wing. I leave a pile of gas cans and a ladder on the side of the runway. I then take off for the mountain strip. This airplane is a little lighter now so I hope it will work it is in the afternoon and hot. After taking off to the South East I stand the airplane on its tail. to get into the cooler air and better fuel performance. I continue turning SouthEast. Now there are too many small mountains. I will turn on my radios and start tuning them to the right frequency and setting in the radials so I can triangulate to get close to the right mountain then I can land. There is another hour or so before reaching the right mountain.

After a while, I start recognizing the mountains and the one I am looking for. The landing strip is on the northwest side of the mountain. It looks like all the radio beacons are starting to line up. A bare spot is starting to come into view, and I am sure I found the right mountain. I am a little high so I will pull the power back and start to slow. This airplane is fast and will be a handful to land on this short of a runway. The airplanes they use here will not go much over 100 KTS. I wanted to go straight in because I cannot waste any gas I need every drop to make it to Texas. My final approach to the runway is slow about two miles long because I want to be able to find the slowest speed this airplane will fly at with this weight and air density. And that's the speed I will touchdown at hopefully the wind is not too turbulent up here. The trick is to slam the airplane on the exact start of the runway not too hard to bend the landing gear and soft enough not to bounce, a bounce eats up lots of braking distance.

I am looking right down the runway now it all looks clear. I slowed down to seventy knots with full flaps and could not maintain altitude so I added some power and at eighty Knots it would fly so I will hold eighty knots till I touch down. It's a good thing the runway is uphill. The runway is mostly rock not sand or dirt you have to be very careful with the use of brakes as rocks can shred airplane tires if the pilot locks the brakes up.

As soon as. I went over the threshold of the runway I knew I was going way fast to stop, so I cut the engine and started using a little braking and pulling the yoke to the stop to help with aerodynamic braking. I look up at the end of the runway racing at me and thinking about going off at the end of the runway, as I did, now the airplane is in the jungle. I turned off the master switch and did not smell anything burning. I am now just sitting in my seat and trying to wind down. There does not seem to be anybody waiting for me so I should get out and check out the damage. The walk around looks like there is no damage to the airplane the jungle here is softwood the propeller was static and did not bend. The airplane looks like if I can push this plane out of here and back to the runway, I will be able to fly it out of here.

There should be someone here by now with some weed. I am starting to worry a little about if I have to go home empty. I am working and chopping the undergrowth pushing and pulling on the airplane. I have it turned around and pointed toward the runway finally. Now it is starting to get dark and no weed. I have the airplane on the edge of the runway it is in a takeoff position downhill. So, it looks like I will be spending the night here. At least there are no seats on the plane, and I can stretch out and sleep well in the cabin. I had some treats and drinks so I will be fine for the night. I am plenty tired now and will sleep well.

The next morning, I am awakened by someone taping on the side of the airplane. I was afraid I would be looking down the barrel of a gun when I opened my eyes I did it slowly. It was a Mexican with a big full-face grin. Now he is apologizing to me like crazy about his truck wouldn't start. I think he was thinking he was going to get slapped around for being late. Now I have to tell him after we get loaded to race his ass down the hill and call his contact to let them know I will be landing at our spot in Texas tonight because of the delay. Also, to have his burro driver watch the trail for me and if anyone comes up that trail to advise me so I can take off early. The plan is to cross the border and land after dark, so I must wait in Mexico for a while and burn some daylight.

I have the airplane loaded and ready for takeoff and I am sitting on a small rise where I can see down the runway and the hill to watch for Soldiers coming and ready to jump in the plane and blast out of here. Walking or running in traffic better get out of my way because I can't and won't stop my takeoff roll. Later in the afternoon, I took off for Texas. I climbed out at a fast cruise climb configuration to minimize fuel burn. I do not have any extra fuel on this trip and there is no way to check the winds. I should be able to make it work just due to diligent navigation. After a few hours, I am approaching the border and descending through a valley to avoid Texas radar. All my lights are off and there is a little Moon and no clouds some low-level haze perfect for me to find my way. The border patrol will have their lights on, and I will be able to see them if they are close. It's looking good I can see for about twenty miles. Some border lights are coming into view and some are small pueblos. No Helicopters or any other aircraft. I am pretty sure we have passed through the ADIZ Air defense zone. Now I can turn on my radio and go directly to my landing airport. Now I am getting close, and I can see the green and white airport rotating beacon. I can see I am a few miles out I put the Unicom frequency on my radio and click the microphone eight times and all the runway lights come on then I circle and land. After I taxi over to a spot behind a hanger and meet a truck and unloaded all the weed.

I flew over to the next town and checked into a hotel we had all picked out earlier for the meet. I had a girlfriend that had a rental car full of pot now in the hotel parking lot. We unloaded our luggage and walked into the room. I laid down on the bed took a deep breath and the phone rang. On the phone was this supper hot lady that checked me into the hotel, she said the FBI just checked in and asked about you and rented the room next to you. I told her thank you very much and told the girlfriend we had to go. Fortunately, we had not unpacked anything and just grabbed our bags ran out of the room loaded everything into the car. We drove off fast and I think those FBI agents will think we are very Quiet. We got out before the feds moved into their room. We must have a telephone tap in one of our friends' lines, we are leaving the state now then we will find out about the leak later. Dave will come and pick up his plane here in Texas in a few days after it cools down.

Now I need to get home sell some weed then fly commercial out to Cali and catch TJ So I can get the rest of the payment for the trip $25,000.

I sold all the weed I had in about a week and called TJ but no answer. I wanted him to send me my 25K but I could not contact him. I called Raymond to ask about TJ he said he hasn't seen him for a while. Raymond said they have another load and he has another friend that has an airplane he will send to Texas for me to use. I told him not to send it until I get paid for the last trip. I told him I was going to fly commercial to California to find TJ to get paid. I flew out to San Diego landed rented a car and went to TJs house he lived with his parents they had a sign on their door that said TJ does not live here anymore. They were very old I did not want to bother them.

So I told Raymond I would not do the trip unless they paid me at least $10,000 of the $25,000 they owed me. He said he will talk to TJ and get at least 10,000 and for me to go to Texas he will send an airplane and $10.000 Cash. Now I am waiting near Austin and on the second day, an airplane arrived at the airport somehow but no $ 10,000. I waited another day and called Raymond he said if I do this run they will pay me everything when I am Done $75,000. $25,000 they owe and $50,000 for this trip. This was crap. I think they thought if I was there, and the airplane was there that I would go ahead and do the trip. I flew back home up North. I am not going to give TJ a chance to rip me off again. When I arrived back home after a couple of thousand spent, I waited for a call to go get paid and go back to Texas and do the trip after another couple of weeks Raymond called me and said TJ got the $10,000 from somebody and then hired another pilot so he would not have to pay me for the last trip. The problem was the other pilot was a Federal. This was too much, so I cut ties with everybody out west for a couple of years.

Now it has been about four years and Raymond calls and says that he and TJ and a few others have been in prison for the last two years for conspiracy for smuggling Marijuana. Turns out TJ was working with a coke dealer whose fifteen-year-old daughter was caught at the Denver Airport with five pounds of coke taped on her.

They quickly arrested her father who they had been watching for some time. The police told the girl's father they will let the young girl off if the father sleaze gives them someone to prosecute, anyone! The father tells the Police about Raymond and TJ and their plan to smuggle some pot. I did not know the coke dealer dad sleaze bag. Raymond (RIP)died not long after that. The story slows down. We are going to Jamaica next. All names in this book are fictitious.

CHAPTER 10

A Plane to Jamaica

I had been making *mucho dinero* but needed a better way to get weed closer to the border and a driver. I only had motorcycles, cars, and trucks, no airplanes or large ocean-faring yachts. I decided to purchase a large motor home. It was built on a Dodge truck frame. It had an all-steel body built by Chrysler and looked like the large class-A motor homes we have today. It was certainly not as deluxe or extravagant but a lot better than what I had been using to move five hundred kilos, or eleven hundred pounds—a travel trailer and a ski boat on a trailer.

I was working with the Felix brothers from a little village near Guadalajara. When I was introduced to them by a girlfriend of mine, they were dirt farmers. I offered them some Sunshine LSD, and they refused it. They knew that I could not be a police narc because I was giving away Sunshine LSD, a class-one drug. At the time, they did not want to leave their farms with large amounts of weed. But in later years, they had made large amounts of money and expanded. Then they could move the weed closer to make it easier for me. The way it started out was that there was a certain amount of trust between the farmers, dealers, and the gringos or me. Usually, they wanted a deposit and would front some of the weed. I had gone into the jungle and worked with the farmers, which brought a little trust. At least the farmers knew what I looked like. These farmers needed the money; their houses had dirt floors, and the children ran around in rags.

One of the things I learned about the ranch life in Mexico was that the chickens ran around the house and kept the dirt floors clean. When you first walked in, the chickens walked through the house to check you out and see if there was any new food. Then, just as soon as they came, they disappeared. My girlfriend told me that whenever new people arrived, the chickens would run away because they knew out there in the ranchos that arriving friends meant a chicken diner.

You could hear everywhere that smugglers got killed for not paying for the merchandise. I started working for the Guadalajara cartels after I first moved to Guadalajara. I was introduced by an old-school friend of my girlfriends. He was the son of, I suspect, a cartel leader. He took me to this large home built out of large blocks, like state buildings or castles. It was in the neighborhood of the Guadalajara Country Club, with a guard at the gate.

We walked into this large home with twelve-foot-high front doors and were met by a silver-haired old man. He was very nice and said, "My son has been talking to you and wants me to meet you." He asked me about what I was doing.

I told him I was lying low from a divorce and was a friend of his son's, and I said I did not like hard drugs and thought that hard drugs were the worst things could happen to a young man. I had no warrants and just wanted to drop out for a couple years. I wanted to find out about getting weed to the States but not hard drugs. I thought that was why he invited me to his home. When I arrived in Guadalajara, I registered at the Institutes de Cultural for Spanish lessons. I was told by my girlfriend that if I had that ID and any police saw it, they would help me do what I was doing and be very friendly. They all were very friendly except out in the jungle. All the medical students have that ID and there are thousands of medical students in Guadalajara.

The old man asked me if I wanted to work for him, driving around some sedans while I was around. He offered me a large amount of money and let me use one of his ranches outside of Guadalajara. It was beautiful. I have pictures. And I could have a horse. I had my '69 Malibu, but they gave me a '69 GTO to drive. My job was to drive around sedans for them. I would never know what they carried in the trunk, but I didn't care. They gave me two guns—one for my waist and one for my boot. But I never came close to using them except playing around and target shooting, could be why nobody ever came around the ranch.

This is the ranch where Kilo John or John Caddy picked up five hundred kilos (1,100.31 pounds). I fronted him, saying that he stole from me. I had been getting tired of bringing weed up from Mexico, and Roho told me about Kilo John and said he would do it if I provided a vehicle. With a name like Kilo John, I thought he might be the answer. So I purchased this large class-A motor home. It was built by Chrysler on a Dodge truck chassis. It looked like all the large class-A custom motor homes of today but was certainly not as extravagant.

I was a journeymen carpenter, and it did not take long to build a compartment that would hold five hundred kilos. John told me that he knew of a border crossing station way out in the middle of New Mexico that closed at night and you could just drive around it.

I made all the arrangements by phone to have five hundred kilos moved to my ranch for Kilo John to pick up. I had been doing this driving from central Mexico to the border for a couple of years, and this was good for me. I felt I could trust these guys; they all called me brother. I felt good about this Kilo John; he wasn't very big and could be taken down easily, but he was called Kilo John! The first bad indication was he wanted me to follow him to Yuma in case he got pulled over—so I could vouch for the motor home, I guessed. Anyway, we were driving to Yuma; and as we got close to the Arizona border, he pulled over on the freeway, ran back to my car, and handed me through the window the ounce of weed with rolling papers I gave him to smoke on the trip. He said he did not want to take them through the Arizona-California produce checks. He ran back to the RV and drove off. As we followed them, I asked my wife, "Is this a good thing?" I was thinking, *What did I get myself into?* I thought about the Brotherhood of Eternal Love. These guys had been giving me all the Afghan-hash surfboards and Sunshine LSD I wanted. What could go wrong? The leader I knew from high school.

Having driven through Mexico so many times, I was almost on a first-name basis at some of the border checks between the states of Mexico. I must have a better way to do this part, so it was worth a try. The first time these brothers had seen a hundred pounds of weed, I fronted it to them. The first time they saw a thousand pounds, they stole it. I kept the families in pot to sell at the *Taco Bell*. Rosey, Roho's wife, told me they did not leave enough money for them to eat and had small children to feed. The brothers did not think their sailboat trip would last for so long. They might've thought it was easy, watching me bringing in tons on my sailboat, the *Kona Mauri*. The only downside was that John would have one of my connections in Mexico. He would meet at my ranch. There was no doubt John will get a telephone number of a good weed connection, but my thoughts were that the more weed that landed in the States, the less often heroin would be used, and very addictive opioids would be not sold for pain.

It's so funny. Imagine waking up in the morning with big back pain after a grueling day of lifting for construction work, and the doctor gives you two choices: hydrocodone or surgery. Or you can smoke a joint, and the pain will leave immediately. If you take a pill, it will be a while before the pain goes away. Now, if you run out of the hydrocodone, you will feel like you died. If you run out of pot, you will be a little sad, and music might not sound as good. But you can still carry on and do your work.

Everything seemed to be going fine. My Mexican ranch foreman called and said my friend stopped by to say hello. That was my signal that John had picked up the load and was on his way north. Now I was thinking I would have a large load coming in about a week. Kilo John's plan was that at night, he could simply drive around a small town he found in New Mexico that had a USA Border Patrol entrance that closed at nighttime. It sounded a little sketchy but was worth a try. About a week went by, and one evening, Kilo John came over with three brothers I did not know or want to know. He told me they could not bring it across because for some reason, a Border Patrol truck with agents was parked at the entrance to the USA at night, and they could not cross it. So they buried the weed. When they went back to get it, the weed it was gone, and they said they would bring the motor home back in a couple of weeks.

I told John, "The problem is if I cannot pay for the weed, the Mexicans will murder me and my family."

He said he would find the money for me somehow. When he came over to tell me he had three friends with him, I realized I was outnumbered, so I couldn't put up a fight about it. It took about two weeks to get my motor home back, and I never saw Kilo John again. I had heard he moved to Hawaii.

A few years later, I found out that Michael and Carol took the weed to Woodstock and found Timothy Leary—the worst thing that could happen—and I paid for it. Of course, Tim moved to California—all the free weed he wanted. It was hard to stay under the radar with Tim around. I knew they got my license plate when Roho told me I should go up to the Idlewild ranch to meet him. It could have helped lead to my income tax evasion case. Roho earlier told me that I could go to the ranch anytime I wanted or even live there. He did not know I had my own ranch. My wife grew up on a ranch and only wanted to live on the coast.

All this action made me think about dropping the brothers. However, I had worked with others in the brotherhood who had paid me many thousands of dollars, like Chuck, and they kept calling or stopping by. I had never worked with Michael Carol or Kilo John before. I went to Anaheim High School with two of them, and that might be the problem. The last time I had seen Carol was in the Fountain Valley house. I have to add that she looked smoking hot. The last time I saw Michael was at a party in Santa Cruse after we brought a Queen Air load of hash into Bermuda Dunes.

I had to pay for all this pot that was lost, and it put a dent in my social and financial life. My overhead was quite high—two airplanes, several yachts and homes, and ranches. I didn't want to go after anyone for lost weed; the punishment for assault or murder was too much for me to even think about. I was into peace, love, and no confinements. The Ten Commandments are good laws. I do not believe that one human being should put another human in jail for smoking a plant that they could simply grow in their backyard and that another human being says you cannot grow (even though God gave it to you).

The Randals had been avoiding me. I called their store a few years ago, left my number, and asked for Michael to call me. He did not do that, so I might run into him sometime. And then we could talk about it. But I didn't care about the money—unless he was really wealthy—because I paid for all the weed, or I could have been killed. The Randals kept asking for donations, but I did not believe it was to pay me back. I do not believe in holding grudges. I believe everything is like water; it will level out

I was getting tired of Mexico, and people had been talking about Jamaican weed. So I started listening. It was started to sound interesting. I pulled out a map, looked it over, and found out that to get there from Florida, you had to fly over or around Cuba. I did not want to fool around with Cuba because I knew of American pilots in jail there. My best shot was to use the route I opened from Texas to Yucatán.

On this trip, I would leave from Texas and go south. Using pilotage, dead reckoning, and long-range radio beams, I would navigate to the eastern tip of Yucatán, then after, I'd have it in sight so I'd know for sure where I was physically. The problem was I could fly out to the Caribbean Sea and maybe have to land on some island with no flight plan. Or worse, I'd have to land in the sea with no water-landing equipment and no rescue plans. At least the airplane would be empty of gas; it would probably float for a while but not for long. Nobody would know I was out there, and I did not think anyone in my crew would report me without admitting they were involved. There were all these all federal laws whenever you had aircraft involved.

I had the route now and needed to pick an airplane for the job. Using all my airplane knowledge and information, I decided on a Piper Navajo/Chieftain. I has six hundred miles to the Yucatán coast from Texas and another eight hundred miles to Jamaica. I would be able to cut the corner a little and save some miles. According to my aircraft performance information, I could add a hundred-gallon bladder tank in the fuselage, which would give me the range as long as I went pretty much directly there. There was no room for miscalculations here. If I brought a thousand pounds of pot, it would put me six hundred pounds over gross weight. I knew that for airplanes to be certified, they must be able to fly at 25 percent over gross weight. That was about what the weight would be at takeoff. I would need a runway that had no trees at the end of the runway.

My brothers from Laguna told me about the good weed in Jamaica and said they had a friend who had been to Jamaica to check out the weed there. So I purchased airline tickets for myself and Squeaky John. We airlined to Jamaica to have a look-see. A few days later, we landed in Montego Bay from Miami. I rented a VW Bug, and John and I drove to Negril on the left side of the road. They called Negril the grill.

We rode around Negril for a while. It was so small in the seventies; it only took a few minutes. They only had one restaurant in the town, and it was more like a fast-food jerk-chicken restaurant. The only place in Negril where I did not see any chickens running around was the restaurant. We checked into a beachside hotel that you will not see on any travel poster. We had a telephone in our room. John called his connection and told him that we had arrived, then he walked off to see him somewhere. He said he would be back later.

I had been reading *Playboy* magazines for several years and read about Playboy clubs, and I knew about the one in Ocho Rios, Jamaica. I could tell it was near me. My hotel was on the coastal road to Ocho Rios, and there was nothing to do here. If you went outside and walked, a bunch of small children would start following and begging for anything. I had seen this movie before in other underdeveloped countries. I would reach into my pockets, pull out any change I had, lob it toward the group, and leave my pockets out for a minute; and after a bit, they would quit. None of them seemed mean or threatening. They were like kids playing loudly and happily laughing at what they got. My change was all tip money in small bills. I waited at the hotel for a while, then I decided to drive over to Ocho Rios, specifically to the Playboy club. I left a note to John saying that I would be back in the morning.

I drove off on the left-side-only road along the north side of the island. It was one of the most beautiful rides anyone could ever imagine, between the ocean and the jungle I did not think there was any traffic at all. This was during the week, so I guessed everything was slow. I thought most traffic came from Kingston, which was south of Ocho Rios, over the mountains and from the other side of the island.

As I pulled into the club, I could see the small parking lot was almost empty; there were only a few cars. I was expecting to see some exotic cars or a Rolls or two, but all of them were just late-model cars. There was no doorman to meet me at the entrance of the hotel, so I grabbed my bag, walked in, and approached the counter to check in.

The clerk was very beautiful. She was nice and sweet in a flirty way. Whenever I used my American Express card, I always got the best-of-the-best service. Most people do not even have any kind of credit card yet. After checking in, I walked out by the beach and into my cabana on the beach. Everything here was dirt cheap. I lay down, took a short nap, and woke up at dinnertime. They had a dinner show. It was not bad. I think the performers were Luis Primo and Keely Smith. I had all kinds of seafood—a very fine diner. I looked around the room, and there were lots of beautiful women. But nothing really struck me as super acceptable, so I went back to my cabana. After a while, I fell asleep. I was big-time tired. John knew what I needed for a runway. He should be scouting for one. I planned on looking at it tomorrow, and if I liked it, we could leave this place and get back to civilization. After breakfast, I drove back to Negril.

I did not see John till the next morning. He pulled in with a couple of guides and told me to get in to go see what he found. We drove out to one strip that was too short and rough for my twin-engine plane. A small plane would've been fine, but not mine. I want to say that when I came here, I did not bring any rolling papers because of customs. Nobody had papers here. I learned how to roll with banana leaves. You just stepped into the jungle and pulled off a leaf and a handful of ganja, and you were ready to roll. It just looked and tasted bad.

This was the second time I had scammed Jamaica, or I should say *attempted to*. The other time, the plan was to leave from the Florida Keys; fly over Cuba, going fast and staying low early in the morning when it was dark; and return late at night, staying low and going fast. Stupid plan, but I have done more stupid things than this and got away with them. The airplane was an old Cessna 402 that had missed many airworthiness inspections. I had the airplane for several years. This time I sent my airplane mechanic to check out the runway. He returned in about a week and said they had about a thousand yards and would have five hundred more in a few days by the time I got there. Most people have never been in an airplane on an off runway, landing or takeoff. It's sort of like a roller coaster for those of us that do it.

So now I had a go bag and no life preserver (*idiot*). If I was going to die, I would. I packed a few things for a few days (water bottle, etc.). Off to the airport we went to fuel up, filling the wings and tips. Next was taxi clearance and then takeoff. I was eastbound. I would fly to Florida that day, make a couple of fuel stops, and arrive late at night.

This was what I believed was fate. The next morning, in my Florida hotel room, I was watching the morning news program, and there was a story about Cessna 402s. They said the motor mounts were failing because of some bad welds, and they all needed to be inspected before any flights. They were all grounded until inspected by a licensed aircraft mechanic. Aircraft logs had to be signed, indicating that the inspection was completed, and then the aircraft would be approved for flight. I had never seen those logbooks and did not have them, but I could do some checking myself at the airport. After I had breakfast, I was going to check out the airplane motor mounts by moving the propellers from side to side and up and down. Then I'd call Jamaica and tell them I was ready.

After I reached the airport, I parked the rental car and walked out to my airplane. There was a nice King Air aircraft parked down a little ways from my airplane, and it was not there last night. This airplane was the one I would use to follow me if I was one of the feds. So needless to say, looking at the dark-blue-and-gold trim on white, it looked like a federal plane and had all my attention. To get to my plane, I had to walk right in front of the King Air. All the windows were covered or dark, and I could hear somebody move in the airplane; I could hear the struts under the airplane move and groan a little. I continued walking up to my airplane, grabbed the hub of the propeller, and moved it one inch from one side to the other, and it moved at least an inch each way right and left. This motor mount was shot. I walk around to the other engine and did the same thing. That morning news show saved my life again.

This airplane had just been hanging on and would be no good on a rough field landing. So I called all the people and told them I would do this another time as this plane would not survive a 2,800-mile round trip. Several years later, I was at that same airport and did not see the Cessna 402 there. I asked one of the fuelers at that airport if they remembered it. One of the guys told me he didn't know anything about it but that that airplane left on a truck.

We had the Navajo all set and ready to go now. I had seen a fine paved runway with locks and chains across the runway, so no one could use it without permission. And hopefully, we would have permission. The runway was not on any air charts.

The guides told me to find it and that if I was coming over the water from Mexico, all I had to do was look for a mountain that had two large *Z*s carved into the side of it. The runway was below it and on the side of that mountain, open on both ends, like cliffs. This was good; I might have to fly down a valley to gain airspeed after takeoff if it was really heavy. This would not be the first time, but it was better than crashing into a treetop or landing in trees or a jungle.

Now I had everything ready to go again and loaded my things. This time I was to fly to Houston. There was an airport I knew of near there that was really large where I could park my airplane overnight. It would be hard for anyone to look inside my airplane and see no seats and a full bladder tank. One of my brothers from Laguna, Chuck, had a band of brothers from Port Arthur, Texas, he went to school with before he moved out west. We had used them several times to pick up loads after we burned out Arizona; New Mexico; and, of course, California. These guys, after working with us for a while, purchased a fly-in resort in Louisiana not too far from where they would meet me to unload the Jamaican grass. They would meet me at the airport I picked out in Louisiana late at night. I should land in Jamaica in the afternoon and return the same night.

I took off early in the morning from Southern California and flew to Houston with one fuel stop in El Paso. The flight was sort of boring. There was good scenery, but it was long. The airplane had a three-axis autopilot. I could just fall asleep and listen to my cassette player. I only had to punch a few buttons, and the airplane would take me where I wanted to go. However, if I pushed the wrong buttons, I might have to swim after landing the plane.

After landing in Houston, I parked away from most of the other planes. This airport near Houston had no tower, but it did have a radio frequency that you could call for fuel or whatever. I made a call on the radio to have the fueler meet me at the plane, and he filled up all the external tanks. I filled the rubber bladder tank in California in my hangar so no one could watch. I was working around the plane, checking the oil and inspecting everything really well, while making sure he did not look inside my plane. It was dark, and he didn't seem to care much. I told him I was just ferrying the plane. I paid with an American Express card, so I was not too worried about the fueler alerting the heat.

Next, I rented a car and drove to a motel. Once I was in a room, I called everyone and made sure they were ready. They should be expecting me to call. I called Jamaica and told them I would see them in the afternoon. They thanked me. Next, I called East Texas and told them I would see them the following night. Everything was set. What could go wrong? The airplane was fairly new and the best airplane Piper Aircraft built, so it should be able to tackle 2,800 miles over water—no big deal. Now I needed to sleep for a little while, but I was so jacked up that it wouldn't be easy. I was really tired already from flying eight hours. I did not need much sleep. If I could get three or four hours, I would be able to do all the flying the next day and night. I knew I could fly twenty-four hours. I had done it before, but I needed some sleep before it started. It would be nicer if I could rest a day, but I could not leave my airplane outside; the way it was set up, it could be tagged and tailed by the feds.

I woke up early in the morning. I found it hard to sleep when so much was riding on the next day, but so what? I ate a good breakfast at the Denny's by the motel, with lots of potatoes and bacon. Next, I returned to the room to take care of a few things and pack, and then I drove to the airport. It was a fairly laid-back airport. If I saw any cops, I would just drive by and wait until later. If they were there all day, I would call everyone, do it the next day, and move the plane after dark. No surprises when I paid for the rental car and fuel with a card. Now I walked out to the airplane with my flight bag and another overnight bag and loaded them. I needed to do a good preflight. I was pretty sure the airplane was fine. I was also looking closely to see if any panel or inspection plates had recently removed or if there were any added antennas or new work on the airframe. It had been out of my sight for several hours after dark, and they could've put a new transponder on my plane or altered one of the two that the airplane had. It would not be the first time I had been followed.

Prior to takeoff, I made an announcement on the UNICOM radio frequency. I mentioned the number of the runway I was departing from and informed that I would be departing the area to the east. I also instructed any traffic in the area to please advise. There was silence on the radio, so there might not be any traffic out east. But I would keep my eyes open. I was going south, but I did not want to advertise it.

Wheels were up, and the air was smooth in the mornings. This airplane was a little heavy. I could feel it. And I would leave Jamaica with a thousand more pounds of the same fuel. I hoped that the landing strip was not too high up on the mountain; density altitude made for thin air and has killed many pilots.

Once I was about fifty miles south of Galveston and starting my climb to twelve thousand feet, the winds up there were from the, and they would help me make up for some lost time and arrive with some more fuel reserve. I liked it. Returning at night helped because the winds were usually light and variable this time of year. I was navigating by the Galveston ADF radio beacon and flying southeast. I plotted a course as direct as possible to a point one hundred miles off the Yucatán Peninsula. As I flew the course, the wind would push me north or south of my course. That would tell me how many degrees I needed to adjust my course by. If I weaved around over all this water and did not fly a straight line, I could run out of fuel. The winds needed to be tracked closely for this fourteen-hundred-miles-over-water trip to be a success.

I had been flying about three hours now, and the radio beacon in Merída, Yucatán, was starting to move the needle around a little bit. Now I was looking for the 090 radial from Merída to come in and the one-hundred-mile DME signal, then I would be able to adjust my course direct to Jamaica. My hundred-gallon bladder tank was starting to empty; so I would have to move some valves, pump switches around, turn off some valves, and turn on other valves with the pump switches so I could start burning fuel out of the aircraft's fuel tanks. Now the afternoon was causing some clouds to build up, but nothing really large. It was easy to pass through the little bumps. It would be a lot different that night. There would be lots of lightning. I would have to tighten my seat belt. The best part was that the Border Patrol did not fly in or around thunderstorms. I have only been hit by lightning once; it burned of all my static wicks and blinded me for about five minutes.

The weather was so nice now. The turquoise water was breathtaking, to say the least. On all these trips, I had never seen another aircraft. I guess when you get this far out over water, there are only jet aircraft, and they were way above me. I was passing the Yucatán ninety-degree radial now and adjusting my course to head directly to Jamaica. Only eight hundred miles to go.

Now about five hours had gone by, and I was receiving the Kingston radio beacon. The Jamaica man told me to look for two *Z*s carved into the jungle, on the side of the mountain that you would see if you were coming from Mexico.

As the island started to come into view, I was too far away to see any definition. It looked like a lot of green mountaintops and no definition. I was still a long way out. I started to descend to stay below the Kingston airport radar. The island was starting to get closer, and I was starting to see something like letters on one of the mountains. A few minutes later, I could make out the letters: two *Zs*. Now I was starting a climb to get up to the altitude of the Plato the runway was on. I was close enough now to see this was a fine runway—all concrete. There was a cut in the trees on both ends of the runway. Now I was entering a modified base pattern. I could land fast into the wind without driving around the island. Now I was on the final leg, and looking at the runway close up, I could see how long it was and all the chains rolled up on the side of the runway. I took a deep breath as I had been worried about this for many days, working up to the last few hours. This was what they used to keep people from using this runway without paying. As I looked around before touchdown, I did not see anyone, and there was no place else I could go without fuel. So I landed. After landing, I back-taxied to the middle of the runway so no one else would be able to land, and I parked and open all the doors. Then I would be ready to do a back-taxi turn-around into the light wind and load when it arrived, then turn around into the wind and be ready to blast out of here before dark. It would be more like drag it out of here.

I was sitting on the airstair door, waiting for the weed and trying to wind down a little, not knowing if the cops would arrive It was not very long (less than an hour) when a small car pulled up. I did not like the fact that three guys were not in a hurry; they seemed to be taking their time. They walked up to me and asked if I was Lefty, and I nodded my head. We all looked stern; and then we all smiled, shook hands, and said hello. And a friendship was started. There were no introductions because of the circumstances.

One of the ground crew pulled out a radio and made a call. These guys spoke English, but the accent was so strong I could not understand him. But I heard the word *gasoline*.

A few minutes later, a gray flatbed truck pulled in. It was loaded with boxes. They backed in through the cargo door carefully. I liked that. They probably worked for an airport. They started loading the plane, putting the boxes on top of the bladder tank. I had to walk over and tell them that I would not be able to fill the bladder tank if they loaded the boxes on top of the tank. They turned to the man I was talking to, who seemed to be the leader. He told me they had all the weed here but that the fuel would not come until the next morning. This was really bad for me. I told him everyone in Texas was waiting for me to land that night. My ground crew's phones were probably tapped, and I did not want to call them and give them a phone number to call for me. Also, I did not want to leave my airplane to go make a call. I needed to cross the border at night with thunderstorms, or I could get caught. I could even get shot down and killed. This threat was always there anyway on medicine flights, but not with odds like this. Also, I told him I would have to sit there most of the day to take off so I could arrive at night. He told me I could not sit there all day since Jamaican navy airplanes flew over that strip every morning.

This was turning into a big problem. I asked him, "Is this going to happen every time I come here?"

He told me, "Now that I know you, I will give you two phone numbers. When you're ready to come back, give me a couple of days' notice, and I will have the fuel when you arrive in the afternoon so you can cross after dark next time."

I told him to move the weed off the airport and bring it back just before the fuel arrived so we could load the weed after they were finished filling the bladder tank in the cabin. Meanwhile, we'd fuel the five other tanks. They asked me if I needed anything, and I said I was good. I had to be very careful with what I ate or drank on these long flights. Smelling fuel was bad enough. I asked him what I should do if the cops came, and he told me not to worry about it.

"If any police come, you will hear gunfire." He told me that if I heard gunfire, to just fly over to that other close airport on the chart, on the other side of the mountain. He said they had control of that airport and only used it in emergencies. "And we will load you there." He assured me again that they had a deal with the police in this area and that they would never come around this landing strip.

It looked like I would be spending the night here, and I was dead tired. Maybe this was best. At any rate, I would know by the next night. I looked left and right. One way was uphill, and the other side was downhill. I gathered my things—my hammock, a machete, and an old Mexican blanket—and walked up the hill to find a hidden place where I could watch the airplane and get away in case the police tried to raid the airstrip. It was daylight, and it did not take long for me to hack out a small area between two trees to hang the hammock on. I had an overnight bag with snacks and toilet paper. It took a while for me to fall asleep; the jungle was not quiet.

CHAPTER 11

Return from Jamaica

I was awakened by the sound of two diesel trucks driving up and parking by my airplane. I rolled up my blanket and hammock, then walked down to the men working on my airplane. They were fueling the bladder tank while piling up boxes around the doors, ready to load. The ground crew was happy to see me. They told me they would be done in less than an hour. I could tell right away these guys had worked around airplanes before. The name on the airline fuel truck gave it away.

I climbed into the cockpit, arranged the charts I needed, and checked the batteries. Then I got out, walked around the airplane, and did a good preflight inspection. Everything was good. The oil levels had not changed after about thirty hours of flight from California. The airplane was almost new and should have no problem for another thirty hours—the time needed to get home. It had just come out of maintenance from a one-hundred-dred-hour inspection when I picked it up. It should be able to make another hundred hours easily to get me back to California. All of the fuel was super clean because the fuel truck had several filters. One removed any water, and another reduced the number of any contaminants that could cause the fuel injection system to fail (not good for over-water flights). They topped off the bladder tank inside the fuselage. Then they worked on filling the exterior tanks. Other men loaded the boxes.

The fuel was topped off, and all the freight was loaded. We were shaking hands and well-wishing. Like in "Three Little Birds" by Bob Marley, "don't worry…everything is gonna be all right." The airplane was big-time heavy, and it is looked like it sat very low; the struts were almost collapsed completely, and the airstair door was touching the pavement. The best thing was that it was cool in the morning, which would help me get in the air. Another thing was that both ends of the runway were drop-offs, no trees to get hung up on .

I was hurrying to get home, so I crawled into the cockpit, working around many boxes and bundles to find my chair. Needless to say, this was a passenger plane and did not have tie-downs or cargo nets, like freight airplanes, so none of the cargo was tied down except the bladder tank. It was buckled in. I could not crash as the boxes would come forward and crush me. The plane was packed so full that there was no room for the cargo to shift much and throw me out of balance. At least I did not have to worry about that. All US airplanes are certified to fly at 25 percent over gross weight. That was not in the airplane book. We were a little over that, but big payday.

I did engine starts, and like new engines, they started right up and idled smoothly. I had to back-taxi as far as possible and get the most out of this takeoff. It was good; this runway was paved. I was sure that if this was a wet-grass strip, I'd never fly this airplane out of here. Taking off on a wet surface took forever to get rolling on grass, and it rained every day in this latitude. I made the tightest 180-degree turn and ended up on the right corner of the runway. I let the torque of the engines take me left, over to the center of the runway, on the role. My feet would be down, on the bottom of the pedal. I could not touch the brakes on this takeoff, and I just enough aerodynamic changes to stay in control. This airplane would not fly out of here if any braking was used during takeoff to stay straight.

The time had come for takeoff. I locked up the brakes and ran the engines to full power for a few moments. To me, this was different from most pilots. Do not fly like me. But at least I followed the book. The book said that a green zone on the temperature instruments area was good, the yellow area was a cautionary area, and the red area, do not exceed. I set my power in the middle of the yellow zone, in the cautionary zone, and watched the temperature needles cautiously. They were in the yellow zone. Even though the needles were in the middle of the red zone for a few moments, I was not exceeding the limit. I wouldn't as long as I did not go past the red line.

The airplane was trying to jump around on the runway with all this power running, but it was so heavy that it was not moving, just shaking. These two 350-horsepower engines were not designed for this amount of power on the ground.

I could see the needles on the cylinder and oil gauges moving up. Now I saw the oil pressure starting to drop. That meant the oil was boiling. It was synthetic, so it could take it for a few seconds. And it had a cooler, so it would cool fast. No red or yellow lights, and that few seconds felt like a lifetime when you were hauling ass down a runway, passing through one hundred knots. I believed that when all these needles met their max limit, the engines would just blow up. I had to catch it before that, and I would like to reuse this ship.

As I released the brakes, the airplane started rolling forward very slowly. This did not make me happy, but it was expected; there was almost no wind this early. I wished I could buy some, but I was in this to win. So I pressed on with the takeoff. The airplane was starting to accelerate a little faster now, but it was still questionable as the end of the runway came up. There was a drop-off over a cliff that led into a canyon.

I was halfway down the runway, and I had only eighty knots. I needed over one hundred knots to lift this load out of here. If I tried to stop now, it would be questionable.

I could go over the end of the runway. It was coming up fast. I had almost one hundred knots now, and the struts were banging loudly and like crazy. I was pushing down on the controls a little—just enough to keep the nosewheel on the ground. Then, as I pulled back on the yoke, the stall warning horn started chirping. The engines were screaming! I was glad there were no passengers; they would not like these noises and bounces and be tightening up their seat belts. Mine was as tight as it could be. I was maneuvering the flight controls to see if I could pick up a little bit more aerodynamic airspeed and keep straight.

I was at the end of the runway now, and I put both feet on the floor and horse this thing into the air. I pulled back as hard as I could on the flight controls, and I leaped into the air for a moment. Then the stall warning horn chirped and started screaming solidly. Then the airplane started shaking and sinking fast. I was not flying. I was falling; the long nose started falling first and fast. It was crammed full of weed, thankfully. There was a split second where I felt weightless with the nose down so low. The plane accelerated rapidly, and, luckily, there was a valley below me

I was descending into this valley now. As I descended and gained airspeed, I was cleaning up the gear and the flaps, and I could feel the airplane accelerating big time now. Since I was going downhill, my speed almost jumped to 130 knots, like, right now. I was going to start pulling back on the power and the flight controls so I would not overspeed the engines. Chances were that the Jamaicans thought I had crashed—until they could see me climbing out of the other side of the valley, then making a wide right turn with a whole lot of noise.

I was now starting my climbing turn northbound. The good thing about these incidents was that they only lasted for a few moments, and you either lived or died fast, no pain.

I finally started flying northbound down low, one hundred feet, till I got out of Montego Bay's airport radar area. The weather was perfect: no clouds, and visibility was, I think, about a hundred miles. The amazing thing was that the air here was so clear; and there was no smoke, haze, or anything like that, just turquoise-blue water and white sand.

I had never seen another airplane out here. This flight was going to take a little longer than the flight down here. The winds were generally out of the north or out of northwest. At this time of day, they would be light this afternoon as the heat built the clouds, and rain would start to fill the sky. The winds would become stronger too. If they were not too strong, I would be able to make it. My plan B was to land in Yucatán, where I could maybe get more gas. The weather last night was thunderstorms after 5:00 PM. Today or tonight, the weather would be about the same as today . I would be there around 6:00 PM.

As I was climbing out, I decided to stay low until I was fifty miles north of Jamaica. I was on the other side of the mountains, away from the airport radars of the Kingston and Montego Bay airports, and I didn't want them to see me leave Jamaica because they might start watching this area more for me when I came back.

Now I was feeling really good. I was north of Jamaica by fifty miles. They would not be able to stop me now. I was starting my climb to eleven thousand feet for lower fuel burn. I was starting to navigate to Yucatán, then Galveston. The air was smooth as I headed out to cross the Caribbean Sea, about eight hundred miles to Yucatán, and I would make a final turn to Texas. I searched around my bag and found my old windup alarm clock with two bells on top. I used it on my ketch and other airplanes. I set it up for an hour, checked the autopilot, and napped a little . After about four hours, I was starting to see the Yucatán Peninsula and feeling really good because I knew exactly where I was; I was not flying somewhere I did not want to go, like Miami or Mexico City, when I fell asleep. Now I was somewhat glad that I had spent the night in Jamaica. If I had returned the night before, I might not have stayed awake that long to complete that trip. What made this route so good was the fact that I had used this runway in Yucatán before to carry Mexican weed to Texas, and if I had any problems, I could stop there. I had friends who would come and help me at least get more fuel for maintenance or give me a ride somewhere if I called. I didn't want to get caught with an airplane full of pot.

One time, I had an airplane problem, and the trip wound up with a bus ride to Tijuana, with no plane and no pot. That's all in another story.

After I turned the corner from Yucatán, northeastbound, I set a course to Galveston by using a radial off the Merída VOR. This would tell me what the winds were doing along the way and how fast they were, and they were not very strong. If they did not change, I would have enough fuel for my crossing of the Gulf of Mexico. They would push further east if I did not correct for them. I needed a straight line, but I would be out of range of the VOR radial after about a hundred miles. But if I used the wind correction I had been using, I should be close to a direct course to Galveston, provided the winds would not change much. After a few more hours, I tuned one of my radios to the Galveston radio beacon, and the needle was starting to get sensitive. It was wiggling a little. This was telling me I was about a hundred miles south of Galveston.

A few minutes later, the needle bounced from one side of the screen to the other and steadied. Then the distance measuring equipment signaled that it identified the Galveston radio beacon and that I was ninety miles south. I punched the Direct To button, and it gave me a good heading for going directly to Galveston. I had been adding about ten degrees to my course to compensate for the winds from out of the northwest. The day had gone by fairly fast. Now at seventy-five miles out, I started my descent to five thousand feet. And at fifty miles, I would be down one hundred feet for the rest of the trip.

I was using my distance-measuring radio now and on a direct course for Galveston, and I was beginning my descent to one hundred feet. The oil rigs were starting to come into sight. The amount of oil platforms out here was crazy; there were hundreds. Everyone could not see them because of the distance from the coast. Now I was slowing to helicopter speeds so that when I got near the shore, the radar operators would think I was a helicopter (I hoped) coming in from the rigs. I could see some of the rig operators in the rigs' cabs, eyeball to eyeball, at the same level, about one hundred feet. Sometimes they waved back when I waved. Salt was growing on the lower part of the windscreen.

Now I was worried about anyone being at the landing strip I picked out. After I did not show up last night, they might think I crashed or got caught. The only thing I knew was where there fly-in fishing resort was located, and I decided to go there. I could not get caught with this load.

Now I was about twenty-five miles out, and it had been smooth flying. I had to alter my course a little to the east, now direct to my spot, and stay away from Galveston traffic. In about fifteen minutes, I had the runway in sight and was setting up for landing. But I saw no one. I landed and taxied back to the end of the runway slowly. I still did not see anyone. This runway was in the middle of a large swamp, and there were no buildings or anything, just a road to and from it.

I sat there with my engines running, and I was in a good position to see the road. Nothing was moving, so, clearly, my ground crew gave up on me and went home. This was probably the best thing to do; we did not want to alert the owners of this strip. It was private. After ten minutes, I took off, flew over to the fish camp, and landed. I taxied off the runway and saw a small parking spot. It looked good enough, and there were not any people around. After a few minutes, a couple of brothers came over, and I instructed them get a truck and unload me. They said that they would not do it here at their fish camp. I could not spend time arguing, and half the load was mine. He seemed adamant about it. I did not want to waste any time. I asked them how much time it would take them to drive to the swamp runway. They said fifteen minutes, and we decided I would stay here with the plane for a few more minutes until I could meet up with the truck at the swamp at about the same time.

I took off a few minutes later, and it worked well. I was just landing as the truck was pulling into the ramp area at the swamp. I parked as close to the truck as I could and opened the doors, and four brothers and I unloaded in about ten minutes and drove off. I started my engines, taxied over to the takeoff area, opened the throttles, and raced out of there. As I was rolling on my takeoff run, I noticed an old pickup truck with two men in the front seat and two guys in the bed with shotguns. They did not look like the police, but they did look mean, ugly, and mad because they were too late.

I flew over to an airport near Houston. After landing, I filled up my bladder tank and the five outboard tanks. I was not worried so much about the feds chasing me. I was going to California and with no medicine aboard. After this fill-up, I could fly all the way to my hanger at the Flabob field in Riverside, California, nonstop. After landing, I pulled my pickup out of the hangar. I used my tug to put the airplane inside the hangar without any onlookers. No one was around. The flight home was easy and boring, but now I was home. The airplane with the bladder tank was hidden in my hangar and ready for the next time. Now I was just waiting for the truck with the load from Texas to arrive and split it up.

One of my carpenters came over with a somewhat crazy idea. He wanted me to open a concrete-boat-building factory in San Louise Río Colorado, Mexico. All my construction workers had a good idea of what I was doing in Mexico. They also knew I had a lot of disposable income. This was not the first time someone stopped by with a get-rich scheme. This time, though, it made some sense, and I loved the sea. I had plenty of yachting time and was at peace on the sea.

Most people don't know about the navy building hundreds of cement boats to carry war materials to the wars. They call them liberty ships. The last place I can remember seeing some of them was in a storage facility near San Francisco.

Being an airplane captain and a yacht captain, you will see so much more than most people can even imagine. Anyone can do it and should fly. Those old ships sitting in salt water for over thirty years prove the concrete concept is good and long-lasting. The problem with the larger yachts built out of fiberglass and plywood is that they break up in rough seas. It started with the catamarans. They do not have a chance in rough seas. I am talking fifty-foot waves. Then the larger yachts plus fifty feet. In the 1960s and '70s would break apart. Sometimes, when the sea is rough, boats get tossed around. Now, the monohull is way better but still needs to be strong. You can see that for a catamaran, if one sponson lands first, you could have big problems. When the other sponson hits the water, tons of stress is placed on the connection between the two hulls.

The cost to open a factory to build an over-fifty-foot yacht the conventional way could be over millions of dollars. My thinking was that cement boats could be made easily for under a hundred thousand. If the boat sold soon after it is finished, I would invest more money into tooling to finish the boat cabins.

I had been moving some cannabis around San Luis Río Colorado and had a home in Yuma. Also, I had recently purchased a Bonanza airplane and wanted to fly it more. This would be a good place to build hours for my airline career. The cement and sand would be dirt cheap. I could have my friend that owned a San Diego boatyard. He had all the heavy equipment to move a large boat. It would be easy to move it on the Mexican highway, which was a good road, all the way to TJ— no overpasses to go under. I would be able to go to work at the factory in Mexico and be back the same day a couple of days a week. I had another idea for the use of the boats.

After a couple of months, the boat-factory idea stayed with me, and I was thinking, *Maybe this could be big.* I had Jimmy, my foreman and a great carpenter and cabinet maker, order a set of drawings for a fifty-five-foot concrete schooner-rigged yacht. My father-in-law was one of the nicest men I knew. He was a rancher and a surveyor and recently retired. He spoke Spanish and knew what to do with a beer. Also, he liked crazy schemes. The only thing was I could not have him involved with my other source of income. He probably knew about it even though I had never discussed it with him, and he should not be in Mexico when the weed was loaded into the concrete boat or around any other nefarious activities.

It turned out my company had built a garage for him several years before I met his daughters. The middle daughter was the life of the party and could shift gears. She learned how to drive using her father's Chevy flatbed ranch truck. Her whole family was the cleanest and nicest of all the people I knew. Needless to say, she drove my silver Corvette Roadster to high school every day during her senior year. Her father, after seeing the 'Vette in his driveway every morning, knew who the car belonged to. He told her if she was going to be driving, she needed to have a driver's license. He took her to get one. I never discussed age with her; I just conveniently thought she was eighteen. I was in my early twenties.

After we were married, I purchased 1967 427 Corvette with an outboard exhaust. It was a roadster yellow with a black racing stripe on the stinger hood. It had 3.56 gears and solid lifters. She blew it up one day while I was at work. She told me when I arrived home that it was in the Chevy garage. When I called them the next day, the manager was a friend and a big Corvette freak. He told me she just way overrevved it and that I needed a new engine. The old engine was a pile of ground metal. It cost a few thousand to replace it—disposable income. I never had a Chevy dealer that did not like cash. I had to tell her that she could not drive it anymore, and she settled for a black Cadillac convertible. She didn't really care about it after that. I got tired of being pulled over by the police for speeding in the 'Vette and traded it in on a new 1969 Malibu with a 350 engine. She was very beautiful and the life of any party. Sad to say, she passed away in a car crash. She's missed by children, grandchildren, and many others. (RIP, Michelle.)

Building a large cement boat is not really rocket science. It is relatively easy for a good carpenter. While we were waiting for the plans to arrive, I was traveling to San Luis Río Colorado to find and lease a huge building in San Luis large enough and whose ceiling was high enough to build a large sailboat in. I found one on the main road to southern Mexico and Tijuana. Next, I leased a new Chevrolet sedan for my father-in-law to drive to San Luis every week. By then, the plans had arrived, and we built and purchase some large tables. Now we could spread out the plans and cut our ribs out for the hull forms.

We were building a fifty-five-foot form out of plywood and lath. When that was all built and aligned, the workers would cover the hull form with chicken wire and steel rods and tie it all together. Then they would hire a cement truck with a concrete pump and plaster the form. They would vibrate the cement as they plastered so there would be no voids in the hull. The hull would finish out to be one and a half inches thick, thicker on the bottom and the keel. After we had the schooner laid out and under construction, I decided I should travel down to Mexico and purchase some freight to load on the boat before it was trucked to the States.

I believed the boat hull, when sitting on a wide lowboy trailer, would be over twenty feet high, and electric power lines would have to be raised to get the boat hull through the highway. They would have half a dozen police officers on Harleys directing traffic around the heavy load. That meant that in any road, Mexican or US, the boat would need a police escort. A wide load lead truck two rigger trucks with 4 riggers, in the lead, two power company linesmen and trucks to follow and lead the wide high heavy load all the way. Also, it would not fit under any overpass in the San Diego freeway and would have to go around them along the way. The me from the power company would move them. As for the canopy, the customs department has covering the inspection station at San Jacinto US border is too low . There was a road that went around it, but it was not close to the border canopy. They would have to use this gate.

My first stop would be Guadalajara. I needed to find out who would have the best and highest quantity of weed available in the next six weeks or so. There was a group of *contrabandos* that had a large new dump truck. It was painted up to look like a Mexican-government vehicle, and I used it before to bring loads closer to the border. After I started flying long-range air-planes, I never used them. I thought they could be government workers in some form, but they had plenty of time to turn me in if they wanted.

I made contact with the truckers on the second day, and the good thing was they said they could secure all the weed I needed and deliver it to San Luis for me. I was considering having them park the truck, which was very tall, in my factory, beside the boat. Using a ladder, they could throw the bundles up over the side, and someone could stack them inside the keel area of the boat. No one would be able to see the loading from the outside. I also had some 4' × 8' sheets of plywood with a thin coat of plaster to cover the weed in case somebody got high enough to look inside the boat.

I left a ten-thousand-dollar deposit and told them I would be back in a few weeks to look over the weed and bring the rest of the money for the load. I drove to the airport, turned in the rental car, and flew back to LAX.

After landing, I drove home, thinking, *Now I can take a little time off to fly around in my airplanes or go sailing for a week or two.* I would fly over to the boat factory occasionally to see how they were coming along and check on a shipping date so I could make sure the timing for this scam worked out. I had talked to Jim at the San Diego boatyard, and he needed a week's notice for the move so he would be ready. Half of the boat mold was done, and we had one more week to finish the mold and a week to get ready and plaster the boat. We were getting down to a couple of weeks to go to finish the scam.

I had to travel charter to Mexico now to check out the weed and see if it was good enough to import. Also, I wanted at least five thousand pounds. This scam would only work once, so it must be big. The next day, I found myself on the way to the airport for an early-morning flight to Mexico. After I landed, I rented a car, drove to a nice hotel, and called my contacts to tell them I was in town and wanted to see some material and drop off some cash.

The crew came by in the morning and picked me up for a long drive out to the ranchos. I had on cowboy boots, Levis, and a black T-shirt and looked like I should be on a ranch. The driveway to this ranch is thirty-five kilometers of paved road. We drove through this large gate, pulled up, and parked with a few other late-model cars and trucks. I brought in a suitcase full of cash as we walked through the large front door, and we were led through the main house and out to the back, by the large pool. Several men were seated around the primo, the owner of the ranch and a large *contrabando* for many years. We all shook hands and gave *abrazo*s, and there were, understandably, no introductions.

We all sat down in a small circle. I opened my briefcase and pulled out bundles of one-hundred-dollar bills. The total was twenty-five thousand dollars in addition to the ten I gave them earlier, which was a good deposit. I had brought the cash in my suitcase, and it was not opened when I went through Mexican customs at the airport. When you flew privately into Mexico, the arrival customs was very friendly and did not normally look into your luggage. I believed they were hoping you were bringing in money. The Mexican economy was bad these years.

After a long lunch, with some cold beer for me and something stronger for the cowboys and the Heffy, we all climbed into a pickup with all-tooled leather seats. It was new. We had me, the driver, and three English-speaking Mexicans that had long guns. We drove on back roads, heading up into the mountains. We traveled through several small villages. No one paid any attention to us. After traveling for several hours, we were getting close to the mountaintops. The jungle was getting thicker now, and the truck was sometimes brushing up against the undergrowth. After banging around for some time, we broke out into this large clearing, and then I could see the rows of marijuana plants that stretched out for what seemed like a mile. We drove up on the better road that wound up a hill to several homes and some camping trailers.

The ranch house had a perfect view of the whole valley. I asked Marco about the view from the air. He said you could see all the plants and everything that was necessary for a huge grow. Marco was telling me that this valley was picked out because it was not under or close to any airways or highways. Marco added that one of the cartel members was a general officer in the Mexican military and could keep all government aircraft out of this section of land. I never wanted to work with the military.

I never wanted to land and be met by soldiers; they would have me without a fight. I had a choice and always thought it risky to land with soldiers around, so why would I? I could choose where to land and had never been caught—the proof was in the pudding. The feds were on my trail now, watching me.

One of the problems was that some rich, politically active executives were driving out to the airports to fly their airplanes on a trip somewhere. When they arrived at their parking spots at their airports, all they found were a pile of seats and gas cans. Their airplanes would never be found, but they had insurance. Now the feds and insurance companies were raising a lot of heat by asking the feds how this could happen so often. The feds kept the pressure up and said there were too many airports that were not locked up, and it was just too easy to steal an airplane. They also said that they had several investigations going on.

After seeing this ranch, I had no problem paying these guys, and I was sure they would perform well. We drove back to the rancho and got out to stretch our legs, and a senorita came out of the house with a tray full of really cold bottled beer. Another server came out with tray that had an unwrapped kilo of grass. The pot looked great—big buds, not many seeds, a nice lime-green color, and covered with a light coat of light-white resin. I had not been smoking all day, and just a few hits got me high and a little nervous. I had never worked with these guys before, but they came highly recommended and had large trucks that could easily move anything. On the long drive back to my car and the Heffy after the beers, I slept most of the way. It was dark when we arrived at the estate. The ladies had a large dinner ready for us. We ate and drank for a while. The ranchers invited me to spend the night, but I refused as I wanted to get home.

I booked a red-eye special for LAX and arrived at the airport just in time. I preferred to fly at night because I could sleep better in a plane than a bed. Not many passengers aboard meant more room, and I could pick up a day. When I arrived in LA, I drove down to San Diego County and pulled into my ranch. I had a Mexican coyote that lived in my barn to feed my horses and dogs while I was gone. He was glad to see me. I didn't know why I kept him around. I taught him to drive and let him use my little Chevy short-bed pickup to practice. He wrecked it when backing up and took out the right rear quarter of the bed. He must have been backing up fast.

Now I was juggling the time around to have the cement boat finished and ready to ship, coordinate the timing for the weed, and have the load ready when the boat hull was ready to ship up to San Diego. First thing in the morning, I flew over to Yuma and drove down to San Luis to see firsthand how the boat project was coming along. The guys down South wanted one week's notice to move 2.5 tons of smoke to the boat factory. These guys were very serious. I had be ready, or I could lose all my investments—and maybe some skin if I told them I could do something but could not do it.

When I arrived at the boat factory, they had one of the schooner molds completed and all the wire and steel stapled to the mold, and five guys were tying it all together and tightening it up to fit tightly on the mold, ensuring a constant thickness of one and a half inches. There were several carpenters working on the newer mold. I told my foreman to pull the carpenters off the newer boat form and have everyone work on the first one. This would finish the first one faster. Then I took Jimmy and a lead carpenter into the office and asked if they were sure they could finish the first boat by the end of the month. It was already the fifteenth of the month. They responded that they had been talking about it and decided they could finish in ten days.

This was all great news to me. Now we could finish the boat without my father-in-law around; I could send him home on Friday. I would tell him to close his hotel room and take all his things home with him because the boat factory would be closing. He would be gone for a couple weeks, before the smuggling started, and should not have to worry about being connected to building the boat.

Everything was set for the move on the first day of the month. I had been in touch with Jim at the San Diego boatyard, and he said he would be ready to go on the first. Also, he had been in touch with the Mexican authorities about the move and the Mexican contractors who would help us move. This move was not the first time a large boat had been moved across the border both ways many times. All the paperwork had been done before, so it only took a couple of days. Additionally, my name was not on any of it, only the company's name. I was set for a move on Monday morning, so I would have to go to the factory on Saturday night and meet my Mexican truckers to load the boat with weed.

I had the keys and opened the factory doors at midnight. There was no one on the streets. They pulled the "dumpy" (that was what they called dump trucks in Mexico) into the factory, then parked it beside the boat. They started loading it with weed. It took a couple of hours, then they all left. Again, no one was on the streets. After that stage was complete, everything would sit till Monday morning, then it would be loaded on a lowboy trailer that was sixty feet long and travel across the desert, over the mountains to Tijuana, then to the San Ysidro Border Crossing. I had a couple of Mexicans meet the haulers and get the boat loaded in the morning. There were several trucks and linemen to lower power and telephone wires along the route. Another truck with riggers, cables, and straps to tie everything down came. Let's not forget the police and highway patrol escorted all the way, even after it arrived in the States. I had arrived home by now and was waiting for the boat to arrive, but I was watching from afar how the boat passed the gate that led into the USA. If it was delayed, I was ready to leave California; my airplane was gassed and ready to take off if this boat was busted.

It was a little crowded at the gate; there were several linemen, riggers, and police (both Mexican and American) standing around to pass through. The Border Patrol seemed a little busy with all the people standing around and were in a hurry to get this over with. The customs agent with a handful of different-colored papers waved the column through.

I left my vantage point near the border, drove over to the San Diego boatyard, and awaited the arrival of my boat from across the street. Nothing could go wrong now. My boat had police protection. I would wait a couple of days before I went there to make sure it was not hot. After a couple of days, I traveled over to the boatyard to check out the boat. Then I called some brothers to come over after five to work on the boat and asked that they bring some extension ladders. All the yard workers left after five, and it was perfect to unload some of the weed there. My Canadians and Texans would be here in a few days, so it could stay on the boat for a few days. There was no rain in the forecast. It took a couple more nights to empty the boat, then I took some photos and put the hull up for sale. I do not remember or know what happened to the boat hull. Legal problems began. *Taxes?*

CHAPTER 12

Landing on a Bridge

This story started when two of my brothers pulled into to my ranch on a fine Southern California day. I was feeding my three horses. I had two Arabians—Akellatez (a colt) and Maratac (a filly). The other horse was a built like a workhorse, and he was a dapple-gray. Raising Arabian horses was my plan. They had a small nose that would fit in a teacup and superthin ankles, just like fine women. The dapple-gray gelding, I don't remember his real name, so I'll called him Spooky. I would see him in a pasture on my way to the airport every day for a long time. He was really a fine-looking animal, big and strong like a workhorse but sized a little smaller. Though, he was a little larger than a thoroughbred. One day, when I was driving on my way to work, I decided to stop and ask the owners if they would sell him. The owners turned out to be very nice and were older, and they said they would sell him for 750 dollars. I wanted a horse to ride and have some of my friends ride with me. After I purchased him, the owners told me he hadn't been ridden for seven or eight years. I knew I was going to eat some dirt by the time I had him settled down. He was like my daughter's Shetland pony; they do not like to be ridden or messed with, especially if not ridden for a long time. However, the horses must earn their feed. When somebody first gets on a Shetland, the pony will try and throw the rider off.

My wife at the time, who grew up on a ranch and was riding horses since she was a small child, always rode the Shetland before Nicole would ride him. I loved to watch. He had more spunk than Spooky. It was like a little rodeo. For a few minutes, Michelle would pick up a stick by the corral and hold it in one hand, and she'd keep the other hand on the reins. The little pony would kick up its heels and jump around for a few minutes, then realize Michelle would not fall off. And the pony would just give up. Then we put Nicole on the pony, and it would act sort of normal.

Spooky was a little different As soon as you mounted him, he would get his head up, go up on his hind legs a little, go down, jump once or twice, then settle right down. This is where you needed to know not to let him get his head back up. If he did, you would probably fly some.

I guess I was a little mean. Sometimes brothers would come out from the city, and they'd want to ride a horse and claim to be a rider. I always let them ride Spooky. I would always warn them that Spooky was a little sensitive on his first ride of the day. Maybe I would forget to say that if I did not know you and wanted to see if you had any metal. I must confess I have seen someone bounce off the ground after trying to ride Spooky. He gave up and drank beer for the pain. I mounted Spooky. He kicked up his heels a little and settled right down. I let the Arabians out of their corral and gave them a little run. After that, I gave all the horses a rub-down and a wash. I had a post in the corral that I tied them to when I was working with one of them As I was combing the filly, I heard running hoofbeats behind me. As I turned around, I went flying up against the filly. I looked behind me and saw the colt was spitting out pieces of my T-shirt. He was a little jealous, I guess, and I gave the colt more time. I had a portable pipe corral that I would sometimes put by my open bedroom window, and he would stick his head in and get an ear of corn or a good neck rub. He was spoiled.

The brothers that arrived that day did not want to ride horses. They wanted me to smuggle some weed and use me to fly it. These were guys I knew through someone in the brotherhood, and I had used them before. They were from Big Sur. I was thinking, *They probably will work for me.* I found out they had another brother from the Big Sur area that had an older 520 Aero Commander twin and wanted to ride along with me to see how it was done. By now I had a reputation in California as a flyer of large amounts of cannabis, which was not good. I always tried to keep a low profile. You see some crazy things in my business. I was thinking, *If I bring him, I will have someone to help me fly the load, unload, gas the airplane, and take the blame maybe? And it will not cost me anything. He will get what I pay for the plane, which will not be much, like, twenty-five or fifty pounds. Another thing is maybe he will help me with medicine without borders. The more weed, the less heroin.* I was not worried about him taking my business. He could have it; I could always sell all the weed I crossed with the brotherhood . I was going to get caught someday if I kept going like this.

The plan I proposed would take place from the east coast of Mexico to Texas. This was going to be the craziest thing I had ever done. If I survived this, I was thinking it would be because of divine intervention or something. One thing I rarely did was land somewhere I had never been, even if somebody with experience I sent had seen it. That was because I had crashed airplanes in Mexico when I took somebody's word for it that the runway was long enough. I pulled out my Mexican air charts and looked for a large paved road that we could shut down for long enough to pull out all the gas cans and pour them into the wing tanks before loading all the weed. The road I picked out was the only one that looked long enough, and it turned out to be a bridge.

I would send two of my brothers to my ranch in central Mexico. Then they would load the weed in a truck and drive it east to the Mexican coast. They would be traveling with a Mexican road crew loaned to me for five thousand dollars from one of my friends in a cartel who would help shut the roads down on the coast. This should be easy because everything going west was checked a lot, but not so much going east. This was the information I was getting from my Mexican cartel friends. They liked me and trusted me, and they had been hearing about me through their friends and connections in the USA. It was also because I did not want to ever have anything to do with the hard narcotics. But I did have Sunshine LSD, and they figured there was no way could I be a cop.

By this time, they had made LSD illegal in Mexico. I did not have much use for it. I had taken enough, and getting caught with any here would cost everything they classified as LSD, like heroin. Not so much with cannabis. Probably my cartel friends would keep me away from the law, and I knew the road crew was armed. But you never can tell. You can get caught anywhere. I will never go into a Mexican jail; I have protection. The place I picked on the map was a highway, but it looked like it had four lanes and was the only one for a hundred miles north or south of the position I needed to work out with my fuel load for the pickup. It was a large road, and it was a paved road, according to the air chart I had. The chart was the most recently issued, but because of Mexico, it could be outdated.

The drivers would look at it when they got there and call me if the selected landing area was too short or narrow for the Commander. The call came, and Doug said the landing spot was plenty long (two lanes), and it was a bridge that was not very wide. He said the bridge had no light poles along the side of it. The lights were on the ground. The wide thing? I was going to have to wing it and hope for the best because it would be nighttime, and there was not enough gas in the tanks to get me back to Texas. I was carrying sixty gallons in five-gallon cans; I had to land somewhere. All I had to do now was give my guys a stack of cash and send them on their way. This was not their first trip. Meanwhile, I could spend about a month or less to wait for a call.

I had a lot of work to do around the ranch, and I have a coyote who lived in a barn and helped me. My ranch was near a casino by Lake Elsinore. My ranch spanned eighty acres. I acquired it through a land contract with a ten-thousand-dollar down payment, monthly installments of one thousand dollars, and the remaining balance due in five years. This was prime real estate—clear and rolling hills. I had no problem. I would have the money in five years. It was one mile off Highway 395, the main highway at the time. The highway ran all the way to Reno from San Diego. I was not afraid of losing the ranch. I knew that if I could keep it for ten years, it would be worth millions of dollars, but I did not think the feds would ever catch me because I had been smuggling for ten years with no problems. I always thought that being connected to Timothy Leary was not a good idea, but it put a noose around my neck. I thought the feds and the IRS had been wanting to shut me down big time, and I did not know they had put out an arrest warrant on me. I found out through my attorneys that they wanted to catch me with a load so they could put me away for a long time and were watching and waiting for years.

A lot of the brothers would stop by my ranch when traveling to San Diego from Laguna Beach, taking the route over the mountains via the Ortega Highway, I think. But anyway, I remember it was around 1972 because that was when they had the first gas problems. I do not remember, but I think it was a supply problem. Many stations had no gas. I could buy gas at the local gas station in Ranch, California, because I was a resident, and I always had fifty or a hundred gallons of aviation gas in one of my barns. You could buy aviation gas anytime at any airport. It boasted a higher octane. I could say it was for my race car. They would never ask, and the brothers loved that 110 octane.

Finally, I got the call from Mexico that the grass was purchased, and the load was on the way to the east coast of Mexico. I called the guy from North California who had the Aero Commander and told him to take all the back seats out of the airplane and pick me up at the airport in Rancho, California. We had all the tanks topped of. Then we drove out to my ranch, loaded fuel cans on my truck, and waited till it was a little after dark before hauling down twelve five-gallon cans full of aviation gas. Then we loaded them in the cabin of the airplane and put the seats in my truck. Afterward we pulled down the window shades and took off for an airport near Tucson, Arizona. We landed early in the morning and slept a little under the airplane. It was impossible to be in the airplane with all the fuel in it; your eyes would burn out before your lungs did. The thing about the gas cans in the airplanes was that after the airplane started moving and flying, all the fumes would move to the rear of the airplane. It was evident because we smoked while flying, and I never blew up! We waited till 8:00 AM for the airport fueler to show up.

The fueler did not pay too much attention to our airplane while he fueled it. Anytime you pull the window shades down on an airplane near the border, it looks very suspicious. Sometime pilots pull down the window shades to keep the airplane cooler inside. I was hoping that no one would look inside the plane. We taped some newspapers on the cockpit's front windows to hide the gas cans and keep it cool inside. I had it parked way down on the end of the flight line. One reason I picked this airport was that it had a nice restaurant. We watched the airplane while we ate breakfast and lunch there and watch TV in the FBO, trying not to talk to anyone and not be noticed.

After lunch we took off for Mexico. I do not remember what time, but we wanted to land in Mexico just before or after dark. One of the reasons I picked this spot was that it was on the coast of the Gulf of Mexico, and I thought I would find it easier at night than somewhere out in the middle of the country. Also, it was lighted. The plan worked out well. I met the coastline about the time I had figured . I had planned to intercept the coast and fly south until I saw the lights. According to my charts, the lights came into view just as I expected.

So I pulled the power back to stop some noise and slow down. We could see the road lights and the town lights a little further down the coast. There weren't many other lights around the area. It was about eight o'clock at night in the summertime, and there was a little daylight and no traffic I could see. Wind was blowing fairly well out of the north, so I knew I would have a crosswind. And the landing area was not very wide for an airplane like this. I took a deep breath and told my copilot not to touch the flight controls, tighten his seat belt, and hang on. Then I lined up the plane to the bridge. That was a little difficult because the wind was gusting, and the flight was getting very bumpy the closer we got to the ground. It was taking a lot of rudder. Thankfully, the Commander had a large rudder that stayed lined up on the runway. I could see the bridge now, and, fortunately, it had a centerline. I remembered that when I got my commercial pilot license, the check airmen told me that all commercial pilots always landed and took off on the centerline. I owned a tail dragger, and my basic flying skills were uncommonly good. Also, I always practiced landing on the centerline every time I landed. If not for all that, I would have never survived this flight.

Can you imagine crashing in an airplane full of gas cans full of gas? After landing and getting out of the airplane, I could see that I had about twelve to sixteen inches of road on each side of the main gear. Then there was a two-foot drop-off to a lagoon. We had to unload all the gas cans, and since the airplane did not have much fuel, we could push, shove, and turn this heavy airplane around. We needed an extra man; we only had the two drivers to help us, and my copilot had been pretty much silent after that landing.

I could see cars and trucks pulling up at the end of the bridge. I got my AR-15 out. If anyone started to drive out here, I was going to lay down a little fire to scare them. Under no circumstances would I shoot anyone. It was against my principles and the Ten Commandments. I couldn't imagine going to jail in Mexico for murder. After turning the plane around, which seemed like it took forever, we started fueling the high-wing plane. I had two ladders and two fuel filters, so it went fairly fast with four of us. The road guards we had tag along were holding traffic, but if the cops showed up, they might run. If anyone started driving out here, there was no way we could take off this bridge or whatever it was. This was the scariest job I ever did. It was windy; we spilled a lot of gas on ourselves and everything we were wearing, working so fast; and watching both shorelines. And I thought God was with us this time, or we would have never survived this flight. When we climbed into the airplane, we took our clothes off and threw them in the back. We had another change of clothes we would put on when airborne if we got up there.

The time for takeoff had come, and I locked the brakes up and applied full power to the engines. When they redlined, the airplane felt like it was hopping around, so I released the brakes.

The wind was out of the north. I had my ailerons fully left to compensate for the wind and torque to help me go straight down the bridge. I knew I could do it with a little prayer and thanks to all my tail-dragger time. My copilot was silent again. I thought he could not believe all this was happening so fast and was rethinking his plan to go on this trip. I didn't think telling him these things happened all the time would help him any. It was sort of true. I always said I would never do these things again, and then I would go down the same rabbit hole again.

As we started accelerating, I started reducing the fully left aileron I had in. I felt the airplane started pulling to the left a little and staying right on the centerline. Now we were almost at a hundred knots, and I had just a little aileron in. I horsed the airplane into the air as it reached 110 knots. The crowd at the end of the bridge must be a little scared as I just cleared them. I was sure it would fly at this speed. The airplane leapt into the air, and as soon as I passed all the people on the ground, I made a tight turn northbound and got out of this area.

Now we started a climb to get the best fuel burn. I had too much on my mind to finish this flight to worry about all the crap we just went through. The copilot was starting to come around and talk a little. I thought about letting him fly us back to Texas now. We would follow this mountain range and the coast north for most of the flight, then, at about a hundred miles south of the border, we would start a slow decent, moving toward the mountains, and use the decent to increase our airspeed. We wanted to cross the border around Laredo. I wanted to nap a little now and wake up when we started a decent.

The copilot woke me. I checked all the flight, engine, and fuel levels. Everything was good. The flying had the copilot feeling better. We started a descent and leveled at five thousand feet about fifty miles out. Then the next step-down went to five hundred feet. We were hauling ass now, and I took the controls and flew down to one to two hundred feet. Then after we crossed the border, there was nothing to see; we had not been intercepted—I hoped. After about fifty miles north of the border, over a small airport, I lined up on the runway, so it looked like I took off from here. And then I climbed up to five thousand for the rest of the flight to Laredo. It was starting to get daylight now, and I asked my copilot if he wanted to do the landing. He said, "No thanks." This kid was pretty much wrung out by now. He was a couple of years younger than me. I landed easily, and there was no one chasing us or any police around the airport that we could see.

We unloaded behind a group of hangars, then flew over to the next town westward, toward California, not far. We landed and called a cab, and we were taken to the closest nice motel. I called mission control and left my number for Big John to call. A few moments later, John called, and I told him where the bundles were. Then he said, "See you in Calli." We got a good night's sleep, and as we were leaving the motel the next morning, I noticed an old Toyota station wagon with California plates pulling a U-Haul tandem trailer, and the rear bumper and safety chains were almost dragging on the ground. I really thought nothing of it until it pulled into my ranch in Rancho, California. Then Big John crawled out. He was so big it took him a moment, then he said, "What a trip." He had backed his U-Haul trailer up to one of my barns, and I helped him unload the trailer. The brothers that loaded the plane in Mexico would be back here in the next day or two.

After we unloaded, we counted the kilos, put them in around twenty-five-pound packages, and went to the casino, where we drank and partied. After a couple of beers, I found a pay phone and called the brothers that were the best at returning the money. Some would get a hundred pounds, some twenty-five pounds or more. Some still owed me money from the last flight, and some moved to Hawaii and did not pay at all. But I was not worried; I would just give those brothers a little less next time. The good thing was I feel safe that most of the brothers would not snitch on me if they got caught. I did not have a collection department. I just hoped the money was not spent on coke.

Some of the brothers were playing around with selling coke. Some took the money and opened a head shop up north. Now some were fighting with hammers and things over coke deals. I knew who they were, and I was trying not to be around them often or invite them over. The cops were not stupid, and I believed they knew who was dealing coke. They watched them and let them go about their coke lives. The cops knew they would slip up, and they would have them. About everyone that was not inside the clique could be a snitch, and I told the brothers not to bring people out to my ranch that I did not know. A few brothers were getting so messed up on coke that if they got caught with anything, they could flip on me and probably get off free.

I stayed out of the dealing for a couple of months and hung out in Hollywood Hills for a couple of months with Cathey and Marty. Sometimes we would drive down to San Diego and stay in one of the rooms at the Kona Kai Club on Shelter Island. I sold my ketch but retained my club membership. Kathy and Marty are two ladies I met at Finian's Rainbow Room in Newport Beach. I believe Tad turned them on to me. Tad was a Korean friend of mine from Anaheim High School. He had moved to Laguna after school and was a brother. He rolled up a joint of my weed and put it in a piece of paper with his phone number. Then he threw it on the stage of a Beach Boys concert. A few days later, I was riding around in Laurel Canyon, smoking weed in my El Camino with one of the band members. I believed these guys thought I might have stronger drugs. I was sure these guys couldn't or wouldn't want to purchase a hundred pounds of smoke, so I quit calling or answering their calls. I did not want to drive or fly up to Hollywood Burbank with one or two pounds of smoke.

Back at the ranch, life was good. I was now settled a little and had a few friends drop by the ranch from Laguna on their way to San Diego. Some of the brothers dropped by today to pick me up to go to the horse races at Hollywood Park. This happened sometimes when they had a plan to move some weed. It turned out they wanted me to fly down to the Yucatán and pick up another load of weed from Oaxaca again. I was afraid to use any of my airplanes because they were probably hot. I agreed to do the job and now needed an airplane. I had one in mind.

I had met a guy from Canada while I was in prison, and he was a smuggler and very knowledgeable about airplanes. He had a friend at the Flabob field in Riverside, California. His name was Bill. He had several cabin-class airplanes that Kenny told me he had used before and would rent me with no questions asked. I drove out to the Flabob field and met Bill. He was a very nice guy and owned several trailer parks in California and Arizona. He was not a pilot and had several pilots that worked for him and used the airplanes to fly around to collect rents. Also, he rented airplanes sometimes to pilots that knew the right people, and he charged a little more than most aircraft renters. I told him I would need the airplane for maybe four days. We made a deal of one thousand a day, and I gave him two thousand, promising the rest when I returned the airplane. Then he told me there was a small problem with the Cessna 402 airplane: it was at Montgomery Field in San Diego, and the left brake did not work. I told him I had a mechanic at Mc-Clellan-Palomar Airport and that if he would fly me to San Diego to pick up the airplane, I would fly the airplane to

Mc-Clellan-Palomar Airport with one brake. This was no problem as both runways were over three thousand feet long. Then I'd have it repaired, and we could start four days after I had the airplane repaired and inspected and leave on my trip.

I had called Michael, my mechanic, at Mc-Clellan-Palomar Airport and told him that I was bringing the airplane to him in the afternoon. Then I asked if he would repair the left brake, inspect the aircraft, have the plane fueled, and keep it in his hangar overnight. I would pick it up the next morning. He had maintained my airplanes and modified some for my many different applications for several years. My wife drove me home after dropping off the airplane.

My wife dropped me off at the airport the next morning, and I tugged the Cessna 402 out of the hangar to do a good preflight, checking all the tanks, oil, and gas. They were all full. This old bird looked like it would probably do another trip. I took off early before the tower opened, and I flew southeast. When I saw Palomar Mountain, I took a heading to pass it to the south, staying low enough to clear the hills and mountain. It was a beautiful day. The sun was coming up, and it was early enough not to see any of the brown smoke called smaze (smog and haze) coming out of the Banning Pass. I altered my course a little so I would see Interstate 10 in a few minutes. I had all my radios and transponders off to hopefully not make any radar images. I knew my way by heart.

I was now traveling low but gradually climbing because I was coming into high desert that was five thousand feet above sea level, called a high desert. That was why it was so cold here at night and so hot in the days (it was closer to the sun). I was cruising about fifty miles north of the border that was not all marked, but I could see it when I was near small cities that were scattered along the border. There were no mountains along this route that were over ten thousand feet, although there was a radio tower in Texas that went up almost three thousand feet. The guide wires went out about a mile from the tower—not a good area for scud runners that did not know the area. I started traveling north a little now as I wanted to land at Coronado Airport, near Albuquerque, New Mexico.

Now I turned on my radios and navigated directly to Coronado Airport. My distant measuring equipment was telling me I was in range. In layman's terms, it was telling me I was about ten or fifteen minutes away from landing. So I called the UNICOM channel and told them I wanted to fuel my airplane and do a quick turn, which meant I should have a fuel truck waiting for me so that after I landed and parked, the fuel truck would immediately park in front of my airplane and start fueling my airplane. I would go into the office, use the restroom, buy some lunch from the vending machines, eat, and wait till the fueler finished his job and called in the gallons. Then I'd pay the clerk; go outside; walk around my airplane, checking all the fuel caps; and then depart southeast.

I started my climb to 10,500 feet now to get into the wind. I was not close to the border and did not care about border radar and climbing fast because the winds generally were from west to east. The winds were blowing over fifty knots today at ten thousand feet; this would be a quick trip to Texas now. I was really cruising along now, and ground speed was almost three hundred knots. My destination was close to San Antonio. They had lots of traffic there, so I would be unnoticed. I would do the quick-turn thing again and make some calls to my Texas crew, telling them I would be close in a few hours and to advise the Mexicans that I would land there the next afternoon and to have everything ready to go.

I was on my way to Houston Hobby now and had been making very good time. I should arrive a little after dark, which was good as nobody would be able to see. There were no seats in my airplane. After I landed in Houston, I could park far away from all the buildings and people. I called for the fuel truck and had the tanks topped off. When they were finished, I checked the fuel caps and rode to the flight office in the truck. I paid for the fuel with my American Express card and no raised eyebrows. I asked the secretary if they had a crew car. She gave me a set of keys and told me where the car was, and I told her I would bring it back in the morning. Then I thanked her. I called the Texas crew and ask them if everything was copasetic.

They said "What!"

I said, "Are they ready for me?"

They said everything was set.

I told them when I left in the morning that I would call, then I said, "I will see you later."

I tried to go to sleep but was worried about wire taps exposing where I was going to unload. Customs and the sheriffs did not have enough airplanes to cover all the airports in South Texas and Louisiana. I was sure all the guys connected to this would be very careful with phones. I was very tired, and it should be easy to sleep. But I was getting all jacked up about the next day. It was almost midnight, and I fell asleep quickly.

The next day came fast. I only got about five hours of sleep, but it was deep and good. I felt great and wanted to eat a good meal and get in the sky. I had the morning off because I did not want to leave too early. The hotel had a restaurant with good Southern food, like grits and thick bacon. I think I drank a whole pot of coffee and went for a run. Sometimes I worried a little about all the guns the Texans had; I could say they were armed to the teeth. If I myself was ever confronted by the American law enforcement, I would lie down on the ground and show my hands. If I was captured with a load, I had a good attorney: George Chula. He was Timothy Leary's attorney and personal friend. He would get me out with maybe a couple of years. If anyone connected to me shot anyone and took someone's life during a scam, they would throw away the keys. I would rather just be shot than go to jail for life.

I drank all the coffee I could drink two hours before the flight. I did not want to eat anymore after breakfast. I would be flying for the next twelve hours, and six of them would be after dark. So I needed all the oxygen in my blood I could get, which meant no smoking. I had two water bottles and no life preservers. It was all over water, but I was starting to feel invincible, like nothing could stop me now. When I got to this point, I felt lucky, and something inside me said, *No shark bait here, and the man can't catch me.* The things I had gotten away with blew my mind. Sometimes I thought they just didn't want the hassle of arresting me and being up all night, dealing with all the paperwork for some pot. If not, I hoped it was because I was not that bad of a criminal. I was just dreaming again. Sometimes I would get into these events where I would just get away, like, right under their noses. I had made this trip several times before and always landed at different airports. It was not so scary as the first time.

Time had rolled around, and it was time to leave. After a good fuel check and preflight, I started everything out. I made a call on the UNICOM, saying I would be eastbound; rolled out on the runway; powered up; and let it rip. I cleaned up the airplane and leveled at eight hundred feet for a couple of minutes, then made a right turn and headed southbound. I would climb to fifteen hundred and stay slow to look like a helicopter. There were hundreds out here serving the oil rigs. When I got fifty miles out, I would climb to five thousand feet, then slowly climb to ten thousand for the rest of the trip. Now I was figuring out my wind correction. I would fly that heading and turn off all radios and transponders for about four hours. It was easy money out here. I had never have seen another airplane out here, and that was good because if I did see one, it was probably looking for me.

Now I would just slide my chair back all the way, stretch out, and monitor the autopilot. I played some music and watched the time. I crossed the point of no return, playing Eagles and the Rolling Stones and feeling much better. Enough time had passed now; I should be about a hundred miles out, and my navigation radios should start identifying. I got a good idea of where I was and computed a heading for the military airstrip we had been using. It was over a hundred miles from anywhere. We were friends with the farmers that lived out here. They'd tell us when the military would be training here. My Mexican friends always gave them all money, and they were very nice. the military never gave them anything.

After I landed, the guys came out of the jungle and gave me hugs and handshakes. Gabby told me he wanted to ride back with me. I had carried several passengers with me before but only one at a time because of the weight.

The others started fueling and loading the airplane. Gabby and I sat down and started talking. Twenty-five percent of the load belonged to me, Gabby Louise, and Pulga. Squeaky John got, Desert, and Skinny each got 25 percent. We all invested cash in it. I was flying it, while Gabby and crew purchased it and trucked it to Yucatán from Oaxaca. Skinny and Chuck would sell it and pay off the Texans for trucking it to California.

I am going to expand on these two guys I call young heroes. Squeaky John met Fat Bobby in Maui when he was very young, like, fifteen. His voice was very high-pitched, so fat Bobby called him Squeaky John. Bobby sent him to Mexico when he was eighteen. I am not sure about the ages, but I will say it was to help with weed smuggling. Somehow he met Gabriel, and they bonded and started scoring the best weed in Oaxaca. I started flying it and never had any idea who was scoring it.

Then the kids, as I called them, wanted to know who was flying it, and Chuck brought them to my house. I loved them. And I am not gay, but they were just kids with hands full of cash and only wanted friends and fun. Squeaky took Gabby to Maui, and he met all the brothers there. He took Orange Sunshine one night and walked out of the Lahaina Hotel with no clothes on, and he quickly went to jail and was bailed out in about an hour. I would let them use my cars and trucks when they came to Southern California.

I had a yellow '73 Cadillac Eldorado convertible at that time. It started raining, and Gabby put the top up when he was going at about sixty-five miles per hour. Squeaky purchased a new Audi convertible and totaled it in less than thirty days. Squeaky spoke perfect Spanish but would not roll his *Rs*. John's father was a professor at Stanford. He had several connections in Northern California. He went to Jamaica and helped me score Jamaican weed. These guys were nuts; they would go anywhere and always had something going on. When I got married the third time, I did it in an airplane. We did it with my Cessna 402 and Gabby's Cessna 210. We had the planes full of brothers and sisters, both Mexicans and Americans. We flew in formation up and down the coast, over the beaches between Mc-Clellan-Palomar Airport and Laguna Beach, during the ceremony.

When Gabby flew back with me on this trip, I think I made it look so easy. We just took off, and he helped me fly a little. The flight lasted for about six hours, and we landed at night in East Texas. We met the Port Arthur gang and flew back to California like all the other times. After we split up the weed at my ranch, I did not see him for about a year, and I found out he was taking flying lessons in Mexico. He showed up a year or so later at my flying service at Mc-Clellan-Palomar Airport and had an almost-new Cessna 210. This airplane cost north of a hundred thousand dollars. I knew his parents were rich, but I did not think they were that rich. I learned he had made the money smuggling weed to Texas. It was a very dangerous, complex, and fast airplane for a private pilot, but what could you say? He flew it in here. He asked me if I could keep it in the hangar for him when he was out of the country and said I could use it if I wanted. I already had several airplanes but not a 210. I used it a couple of times to go get parts in Los Angeles, but I did not want to take it out of the country. The Cessna 210 was the fastest single-engine plane that Cessna built for sale. To make it faster, it had a turbo charger, which made it more complex and not good for a private pilot. The main problem was it could be overboosted on the ground at takeoff. It was not running too well the next time he came in. I told him he should have it looked at, but he did not want to. And I did not want to fly it myself. The engine missed a little; it was just not as smooth as it should be. This could be caused by overboosting several times, which could cause cylinders to fail. Sadly, the engine did fail on takeoff on a trip to pick up another load in Mexico, and he did not survive. Squeaky John died a couple of years later in Georgia. It could have been an overdose.

*****

This book was not written to glorify drugs. It shows the dangers that accompany drug use and smuggling. Many of my best friends and brothers have been murdered or died from overdoses, suicides, and airplane crashes that were not mentioned in the book until now. So far, all the movers-and-shakers brothers that I have known and worked with are gone. There are a few that rolled up some hash in carpets and shipped them that are running or walking around, saying that they are great smugglers. But all the ones known to me that carried grass or hash across a border are gone, like Mad Dog, Kilo John, Gearloose

Bill, Smitty, Gabby, Dan D., and many more. (RIP to all.) The last two were in airplanes, doing the work.

The criminals here are Big Pharma, Big Alcohol, and Big Tobacco. One human being incarcerating another human being for a very small amount of a God-given substance goes against everything that is right in the world. There is good to be seen here if one has an open mind. The best high is all natural, if that is what you are looking for, but there are many physical and mental conditions that require cannabis or LSD. After all this, I believe they are not to be used for recreation. An all-natural high is the highest and always the best! Nowadays, with good food, good drink, and good thoughts, everyone can live to be over a hundred years old.

ALL PICTURES

Sunshine Ranch

Hippy Vaquero

Selling beer along the German Poland border Cold War.

Mom saying goodbye.

Clubbing in Mexico

Camping with 500 pounds.

Kona Mauri Documented Vessel

Cruising

After a long trip

Loving the weather down south

Painting boat hull

South bound cleaning gear

This is hard work

My first airplane.

My Fastest Little Twin

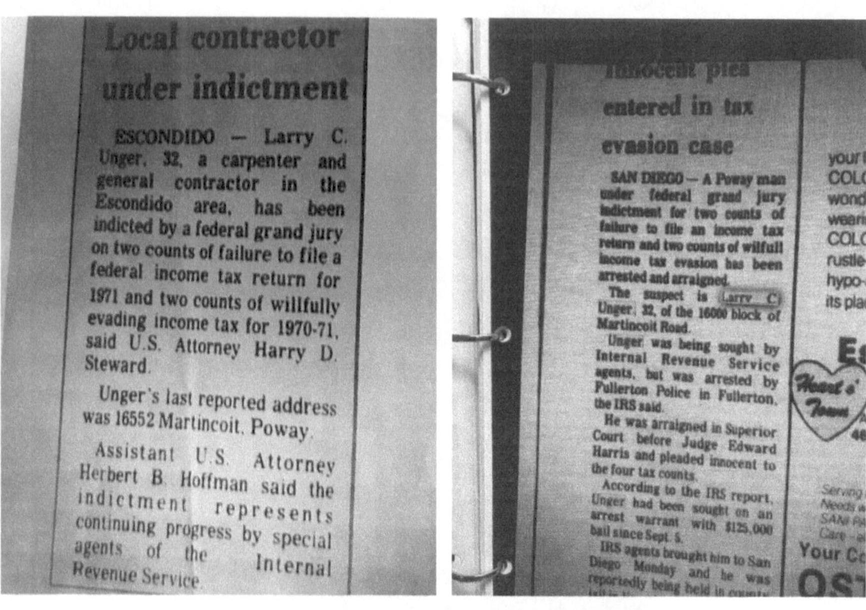

Local contractor under indictment

ESCONDIDO — Larry C. Unger, 32, a carpenter and general contractor in the Escondido area, has been indicted by a federal grand jury on two counts of failure to file a federal income tax return for 1971 and two counts of willfully evading income tax for 1970-71, said U.S. Attorney Harry D. Steward.

Unger's last reported address was 16552 Martincoit, Poway.

Assistant U.S. Attorney Herbert B. Hoffman said the indictment represents continuing progress by special agents of the Internal Revenue Service.

Innocent pleas entered in tax evasion case

SAN DIEGO — A Poway man under federal grand jury indictment for two counts of failure to file an income tax return and two counts of willfull income tax evasion has been arrested and arraigned.

The suspect is Larry C. Unger, 32, of the 16000 block of Martincoit Road.

Unger was being sought by Internal Revenue Service agents, but was arrested by Fullerton Police in Fullerton, the IRS said.

He was arraigned in Superior Court before Judge Edward Harris and pleaded innocent to the four tax counts.

According to the IRS report, Unger had been sought on an arrest warrant with $125,000 bail since Sept. 5.

IRS agents brought him to San Diego Monday and he was reportedly being held in count...

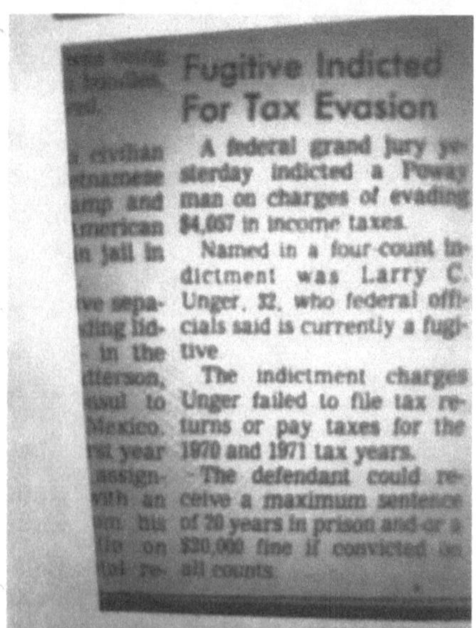

Fugitive Indicted For Tax Evasion

A federal grand jury yesterday indicted a Poway man on charges of evading $4,057 in income taxes.

Named in a four-count indictment was Larry C. Unger, 32, who federal officials said is currently a fugitive.

The indictment charges Unger failed to file tax returns or pay taxes for the 1970 and 1971 tax years.

The defendant could receive a maximum sentence of 20 years in prison and/or a $20,000 fine if convicted on all counts.

Three newspaper articles that were published by a newspaper in California that has been out of business for over 10 years.

About the Author

Larry Unger was a rebel raised in Orange County's Anaheim, California, in the 1950s, 1960s, and 1970s, a soldier, a sailor, a motorcyclist, fugitive and an airline pilot who lived fast and is now enjoying the retired life in Florida. Larry was blessed with a life full of children and grandchildren and enjoys the beach and writing about wild times and distant memories.